DRONES

AND THE ETHICS OF TARGETED KILLING

DRONES

AND THE ETHICS OF TARGETED KILLING

Kenneth R. Himes, OFM

PENTAGON PRESS

DRONES AND THE ETHICS OF TARGETED KILLING

Kenneth R. Himes, OFM

ISBN 978-81-8274-935-1

First Indian Edition 2017

First published in United States in 2016 by **Rowman & Littlefield,** A wholly owned subsidiary of **The Rowman & Littlefield Publishing Group, Inc., 4501 Forbes Doulevard, Suite 200, Lanham Maryland 20706**. This edition published in arrangement.

Published in India by
PENTAGON PRESS
206, Peacock Lane, Shahpur Jat
New Delhi-110049
Phones: 011-64706243, 26491568
Telefax: 011-26490600
email: rajan@pentagonpress.in
website: www.pentagonpress.in

Printed at Aegean Offset Printers, Greater Noida, U.P.

For my students
at the Washington Theological Union 1980–2003
and at Boston College 2004 to the present

It has been a pleasure (at least for me).

CONTENTS

LIST OF ACRONYMS

AFB	air force base
AQAP	al-Qaida in the Arabian Peninsula
AUMF	Authorization for the Use of Military Force
BIJ	Bureau of Investigative Journalism
CIA	Central Intelligence Agency
DARPA	Defense Advanced Research Projects Agency
DPH	direct participation in hostilities
FISA	Foreign Intelligence Surveillance Act
HVT	high-value target
ICRC	International Committee of the Red Cross
IDF	Israel Defense Forces
JSOC	Joint Special Operations Command
LWJ	Long War Journal
MAM	military-age male
NAF	New America Foundation
PA	Palestinian Authority
PFLP	Popular Front for the Liberation of Palestine

PLO	Palestine Liberation Organization
POW	prisoner of war
RPA/RPV	remotely piloted aircraft (or vehicle)
UAV	unoccupied (or unmanned) aerial vehicle
WMDs	weapons of mass destruction

PREFACE

On September 30, 2011, Anwar al-Awlaki, a Muslim cleric and a native-born American citizen, died in northern Yemen. Mr. Awlaki was killed by a CIA drone attack in which he was the specific target. The stated reason for the U.S. government's deliberate killing of one of its own citizens was that Awlaki was an active leader of al-Qaida in the Arabian Peninsula. Mr. Awlaki appears to be the first U.S. citizen that our government has publicly targeted for killing. Reactions to his death ranged from praise for another Obama administration success in the fight against terrorists to condemnation of Obama's decision to approve the extrajudicial killing of a fellow American.

One critic challenged those on the political left who criticized the Bush administration's counterterrorist policies yet support Obama's actions. Glenn Greenwald of Salon.com raised the issue of a double standard, suggesting that if the Bush White House had a "hit list" there would be Democratic anger everywhere. Yet the reaction of many Obama voters was muted. He asked, "If you're willing to endorse having the White House functionaries meet in secret—with no guidelines, no oversight, no transparency—and compile lists of American citizens to be killed by the CIA without due process, what aren't you willing to support?" For good measure he also added, "Remember, good Democrats hate the death penalty because they think it's so terribly barbaric to execute people whose guilt is in doubt (even if, unlike Awlaki, they've enjoyed an indictment and full jury trial, lawyers, the right to examine evidence and to confront witnesses, multiple appeals, and habeas petitions)."

As one who usually finds himself on the political left, is a member of the Democratic Party, voted for Obama in two presidential elections, and opposes the death penalty, I thought, just maybe, Mr. Greenwald was talking to me. And so I went back to a file I had started in preparation for a class presentation in a course on the ethics of war and peace that I have taught for many years. The presentation was to be on targeted killing, but it was never given since students enrolled in the course were given a choice of topics to be included in the syllabus and targeted killing did not make the cut.

Since then drones have become a major topic of controversy in the United States and around the world. A simple Google search on "drone warfare" produced 7,630,000 items. While much of this attention is all to the good—trying to promote understanding of the topic and bringing policy discussion about drones out into the open—the attention can be misleading. Drones raise some new issues for the ethics of killing, but many of the questions that are being asked about drone warfare pertain to another broader topic of which drones are but a piece.

Many questions asked about the use of drones for lethal attacks have been asked before and are not occasioned for the first time by the growing use of drones. Instead, the questions have been voiced in various forms during earlier debates about aerial bombardment and other weapons that permit remote killing. One aim of this study is to return to some of those prior debates to gain perspective on the present discussion of drone warfare. My main contention is that drone attacks are a species of the genus of human action called targeted killing. Clarity about the morality of targeted killing in general will assist in an ethical assessment of the particular use of drones in counterterrorist activity.

Drones, or remotely piloted air vehicles, have become an iconic tool of contemporary armed conflict. Without question an armed drone is a powerful weapon. The combat value of drone strikes is clear and is the main reason for the rapid expansion of their use. However, to what degree is the use of armed drones ethical? How might a reliance on current and future drones challenge the appropriate management of war in ways that will prove to be highly negative, even for those who strongly support their current use? Certainly the history of military technology and warfare is filled with cases where what was clearly valuable from one perspective turns out to be a terrible mistake some years later—and, often, a grave ethical failure.

War is always action involving profound moral questions. It is useful and sobering to reflect upon our current drone policy using the guidance of a moral tradition. A moral tradition situates contemporary ethical debates within a perspective that gives us critical distance from our immediate situation, allowing us to draw upon the collective wisdom of generations before us. The discussion of ethics in war has evolved over centuries and those developments can help us reflect upon the death and destruction that come with armed conflict.

Perhaps the best known tradition of moral reasoning about armed conflict is the just war tradition. While there are a number of different theories of just war within the broad moral tradition, what permits these various theories to be considered a tradition is that they share a "family resemblance." That resemblance distinguishes them from other critical approaches to warfare. All theories within the just war tradition share fundamental tenets that set them apart from pacifist (all war is morally wrong) or purely pragmatic (do whatever it takes to win) viewpoints on warfare. Any theory of just war maintains that (1) war is subject to ethical analysis; (2) war is justifiable for at least one cause and in at least one circumstance; and (3) moral norms can and should be devised to govern the decision to wage war as well as how to conduct a war. The pacifist tradition challenges the second point and a purely pragmatic approach to waging war disagrees with the third point and possibly the first.

As drones come to play a greater role in our current conflicts, it is incumbent upon our democratic society to engage in moral reasoning as well as legal, strategic, and political thought concerning armed drones. For those who stand within the just war tradition there is an obligation to assess why we go to war, but also to consider the moral dimensions of how to act when at war. Should one accept the rightness of the decision for the United States to initiate a military campaign against international terrorism, there must still be a judgment passed on the means employed in that campaign.

Part of this process requires that we ask ourselves a variety of questions. Armed drones raise difficult questions—moral questions that cannot be offset by expediency and efficiency. Engaging the drone policy of the United States from a moral perspective is one of the core challenges of our time. Much of the debate surrounding drone use has been provided by lawyers. There are legal questions about how the Bush and Obama administrations have used drones and whether there is proper legal authorization for the policies under domestic law and whether those policies are within the framework of international law. I am not a lawyer, and while I have learned a great deal from the legal analyses that I have studied, it is not the legality but the morality of drone use that is the focus of this book. As a Catholic theologian I am convinced that any positive law must be judged by a higher moral law. And so it is the ethical perspective that is foremost in what follows. Of course, one does not have to hold religious beliefs to believe there is a moral law that has primacy over the existing law of a nation or nations.

A word about the style and format of the volume is necessary. Throughout the book I often use abbreviations or acronyms after the first use of an expression or organization. I have chosen to use "drones" to describe the aircraft that are also designated by the acronyms UAVs (unmanned aerial vehicles) or the preferred air force term, RPVs (remotely piloted vehicles). This is due solely to the fact that despite the commonality of UAV or RPV in academic and government literature, the word "drone" remains the term most used in popular discourse.

Another decision was to refer to the terrorist organization once led by Osama bin Laden as "al-Qaida." There have been various English spellings of the group and that is reflected in the sources referenced for this book. For the sake of consistency I have changed even direct quotations so that al-Qaida is the spelling used throughout the book.

The overall trajectory of the book is to first examine some past contexts that will inform my consideration of how U.S. policy on armed drones should develop in the future. Chapter 1 presents introductory remarks concerning targeted killing and how the expression is to be understood. It is important to clarify the language used to describe lethal acts, for I have found dozens of examples in the literature of authors talking past one another or confusing issues by the way that words are used without clarification. The chapter also provides essential background information about drones and clears up common misconceptions.

The next four chapters examine four contexts that help in devising a moral assessment of drone use in targeted killing. Chapter 2 takes a look at the distant context of how targeted killing has been treated throughout the centuries, including in the Bible and in classical Greek and Roman literature. Then in chapter 3 there is a study of the proximate context, a vibrant debate that took place among Israelis over the public announcement of the state of Israel's practice of targeted killing at the time of the second Intifada. Chapter 4 moves the investigation into the immediate context of the Obama administration's policy and the rationale provided to justify it. Finally, in chapter 5, I suggest the future context for drone killing by organizing the central issues for a moral assessment under a variety of headings and presenting my thoughts about each of them. It is my hope that even if a reader disagrees with my conclusions I will have provided the information and identified the concerns in a way that is helpful for moral reflection.

In closing I want to acknowledge Tate Krasner, who provided much helpful research as well as good cheer during his time as my undergrad research assistant. In addition I wish to thank Sarah Stanton, my editor, and all the production staff at Rowman & Littlefield whose labors have brought my original manuscript to publication.

I

UNDERSTANDING TARGETED KILLING AND DRONES

On March 7, 2013, Sulaiman Abu Ghaith, a son-in-law of Osama bin Laden, was arrested at an airport in Jordan and placed in American custody. As a result he became part of a select group: a high-level terrorist suspect who was not killed by American forces when found. As one report described him, Abu Ghaith was "a rare illustration of what Obama administration officials have often said is their strong preference for capturing terrorists rather than killing them."[1] Despite that stated preference, however, there have been far more killings of terrorist suspects than there have been arrests of such individuals. The ratio of killing to capture is roughly 30 to 1. In short, "killing is more convenient than capture for both the United States and the foreign countries" where the suspects are located.[2]

Following the attacks of 9/11, the United States adopted a policy of targeted killing (often abbreviated "TK") as a key element in the war against terrorists. Both the U.S. military and the Central Intelligence Agency have engaged in the practice of targeted killing. The military used it as part of combat operations in Afghanistan and Iraq; the CIA has followed the practice in its antiterrorist strategies in Pakistan, Yemen, and Somalia. While the availability of drones has surely encouraged an expansion of the practice, it is an error to equate targeted killing with drone attacks. In modern times, sniper fire, cruise missiles, Special Ops attacks, helicopter gunships, poisonings, car bombs, and other explosive devices have all been used in targeted killings, even if the Obama administration is increasingly reliant upon the employment of drones for carrying out its policy. Understanding the practice of targeted killing is important since it is likely to grow as an element of U.S. military policy for reasons that will be explained in this chapter.

THE LANGUAGE OF KILLING

Steven David, an Israeli political philosopher who has written extensively on the topic, defines targeted killing as "the intentional slaying of a specific individual or group of individuals undertaken with explicit government approval."[3] The United Nations Special Rapporteur on extrajudicial, summary, or arbitrary executions has added additional nuance, defining targeted killing as "the intentional, premeditated and deliberate use of lethal force, by States or their agents acting under colour of law, or by an organized armed group in armed conflict, against a specific individual who is not in the physical custody of the perpetrator."[4] So targeted killing is not an action by private individuals but agents of a state or a party in armed conflict. It is not accidental or random and the victim is not under the control of the killer. The use of targeted killing also claims to satisfy an authorized legal standard.

The term *targeted killing*, however, is not defined by international law. It was first used in 1986 by the human rights group Americas Watch to differentiate the killings of specific individuals by Salvadoran death squads from random killings done by those same death squads during that nation's civil war.[5] The expression came to greater prominence in 2000 during the second Intifada as part of the state of Israel's policy of counterterrorism.

Many moral traditions, including the vast majority of authors within the Jewish and Christian traditions, permit the taking of life under specific circumstances. A simple but important distinction is between murder and killing. Killing is the taking of a life, and when done to a human being it is homicide. Murder is understood as unjust killing or homicide.

All murders are killings but not all killings are murders because some killings are not viewed as being unjust by the majority of commentators in these traditions.

One error in the present debates is the use of ethically loaded language to describe targeted killing. That is, expressions like "murder" are used to describe targeted killing, which only begs the question to be examined. Are all targeted killings unjust or may there be morally justifiable targeted killings? Describing targeted killing as "extrajudicial killing," linking the practice to the tragic deaths of the many victims of repressive regimes in Central and South America during the 1970s and 1980s, is another example of ethically loaded language.[6] Perhaps the most commonly used word as an equivalent for targeted killing is that of "assassination," a particular species of killing that has been debated throughout the centuries. Assassination figures prominently in the debate over targeted killing because many critics cite both domestic and international law prohibiting assassination. So if targeted killing is presumed to be the equivalent of assassination, the critics claim it violates established legal norms.

Assassination and Targeted Killing

Although widely practiced in different historical eras, assassination is now commonly viewed negatively[7] and so is banned by international treaty.[8] It is also proscribed by customary law. Both Hugo Grotius in the seventeenth century and Emer de Vattel in the eighteenth century, forerunners of modern international law, viewed assassination as a violation of the norms of statecraft.

In the modern lexicon of killing, assassination has a pejorative connotation due to its being linked with treachery and perfidy. In 1863, the U.S. Army adopted the Lieber Code, which referred to assassination as "barbarism." The Hague Conference of 1907 formulated a treaty that forbade combatants in "armed conflict" from killing another "treacherously," a code word for assassination. In a similar vein, Brian Johnstone has argued that the Christian moral tradition distinguishes between assassination and tyrannicide by treating assassination as a particular *way* of committing tyrannicide, one that involves unacceptable means, that is, treachery, perfidy. By his reading, the tradition allows tyrannicide under certain conditions, but bans the use of treacherous means.[9]

Closer to our own time and place, the Church and Pike committees, parallel Senate and House investigations of CIA activity during the decades of the 1950s and 1960s, exposed and strongly condemned American assassination plots against Patrice Lumumba of Congo, Fidel Castro of Cuba, and other political leaders. The outrage resulting from those revelations led President Gerald Ford to issue an executive order in 1976 that prohibited assassination or conspiracy to commit assassination by any employee of the U.S. government. In 1978 Jimmy Carter expanded the ban to all those acting on behalf of the U.S. government, whether employed or not. Every successive president, including Barack Obama, has reaffirmed Executive Order 12333.[10]

However, U.S. law prohibits government-sponsored assassination only in peacetime. International law also assumes the assassin is acting in peacetime on behalf of a state and not as a private individual. Both the domestic and international laws prohibiting assassination still permit attacks upon specific individuals of an enemy regime in time of war as long as the person is an active participant in the military chain of command. So the legal ban on assassination does not pertain to military acts in the context of armed conflict, which is why the issue of American forces carrying out targeted killings to combat terrorism is hardly settled, or even clarified, by calling them assassinations.

Assassination in peacetime is generally seen as a particular form of murder. Some so-called assassinations are simply unjust killings carried out by private individuals without government authorization and amount to little more than politically motivated murder, for example, the deaths of John F. Kennedy, Martin Luther King, Jr., and Robert F. Kennedy.

The absolute wrongfulness of assassination is not self-evident, however. Not all assassinations necessarily entail treacherous or perfidious activity. The crucial moral factor would seem to be less a matter of betrayal or disloyalty and more the rightness of the premeditated, deliberate killing of a specific individual. Why is the specific victim targeted? And what justification can be given for overriding the strong presumption against taking a life? History testifies to a broad range of answers given in response to those questions, with not all the answers leading to the conclusion that a given assassination was wrong.

In the case of attempts upon Adolf Hitler's life, the crucial moral factor would seem to have been less a matter of betrayal, or disloyalty, or unjust trickery, and more the rightness or wrongfulness of a premeditated, deliberate killing of a specific individual for political purposes. Traditionally, the tests have been: what is the character of the targeted leader, what is the character of the regime, and are there political options available to bring about needed change without assassination? In the case of Hitler there were morally serious people of sensitive conscience who thought assassination possible.[11]

Some clarity about terminology is needed then, even if the distinctions are only stipulated for this book. Assassination, as I will employ the term, is understood to be a targeted killing done in peacetime, by an authorized agent of a state, and for a political motive. Therefore, a targeted killing during armed conflict is not assassination: snipers are not assassins; a targeted killing by a private individual is not assassination: a Mafia hit man is not an assassin; a targeted killing done for financial gain is not assassination: a drug dealer killing another dealer is not an assassin.

Due to the lack of precision in terminology and, as chapter 2 will demonstrate, the varying viewpoints regarding assassination, its usage as a description of targeted killing does not serve to clarify the ethical assessment. Some, though not all, targeted killings may be termed assassination in the sense prohibited by U.S. and international law, yet there are acts of targeted killing not accurately described as assassinations in the legal sense. It is these targeted killings that will be examined in the U.S. policy of counterterrorism.

Some assassinations, however, are acts of targeted killing. Whether they are legally permissible and/or morally licit has long been a topic of debate. As noted above, peacetime assassination has been prohibited in the United States since the 1970s and is opposed on ethical grounds by many commentators. But there have been periods in times past when assassinations have been legal and defended on moral grounds, as will be discussed in the next chapter. So targeted killing may include some assassinations, though not all, and targeted killing also includes other lethal actions not accurately described as assassinations.

TARGETED KILLING TODAY

Of course, the phenomenon of targeted killing is nothing new. As one former government official put it, "strategic manhunts themselves are almost as old as organized warfare itself." We know that Alexander the Great sought the defeated Persian ruler, Darius III, from Mosul to eastern Iran and the ancient Romans targeted Hannibal as he fled after the Second Punic War.[12]

It was the Israeli policy of targeted killing directed at Palestinian militants, acknowledged in 2000, that occasioned the first sustained and public debate about the morality of targeted killing. That debate will be examined in chapter 3. Since the terror attacks on U.S. soil in 2001, it is the U.S. policy of targeted killing that has now moved to center stage in the debates about the ethics of the practice.

On September 17, 2001, George W. Bush signed a still classified presidential directive that delegated to the CIA the authority to conduct targeted killings. Although it is difficult to know with exactitude the death count, since there are no official figures given by any side involved, many informed commentators estimate there have been over four thousand people killed by targeted killing in Pakistan, Somalia, and Yemen, places where we are not involved in a declared war. If the number of those killed as a result of targeted killing in the war zones of Afghanistan and Iraq were added to the total dead, the number would be considerably higher.

Right after 9/11 the policy was focused on "high-value targets" (HVTs), terrorists perceived to be significant actors in al-Qaida. With the invasion of Iraq the practice of targeted killing greatly expanded. The U.S. military undertook a strategy of terrorist hunting through the activities of the Joint Special Operations Command (JSOC). These Special Operations forces became crucial to the counterterrorism policy of the United States. Under the leadership of Gen. Stanley McChrystal, the JSOC developed an approach similar to that of the CIA's Phoenix program during the Vietnam War. In night raids upon homes of suspected terrorists, the American forces would either kill or capture their targets and then scour phones and computers for further intelligence about the insurgency.[13]

One significant difference between the strategy pursued by JSOC and that of the CIA in Vietnam is that the counterterrorism campaign in Iraq soon grew to the point that the borders of the battlefield extended far beyond the declared war zone of Iraq. The Taliban in Afghanistan were also a target for McChrystal's forces and soon targeted killing was extended to Pakistan, which was providing safe havens for the Taliban leadership. In the latter case, however, it was not ground troops carrying out the targeted killing but armed drones. During George W. Bush's presidency there were four dozen drone strikes in Pakistan. As of early 2015, Barack Obama has authorized more than four hundred strikes by the CIA in Pakistan, Somalia, and Yemen.

Targeted killing is likely to continue for a variety of reasons. First, many nations, including the United States, have a tendency to "personalize" conflicts. Whether it is Castro, Ho Chi Minh, Qaddafi, bin Laden, or another leader, there is a need to rally public support in a conflict and that is often helped if a specific villain can be named and targeted. Second, as the weapons of war have become more destructive, the communications technology that brings the effects of war home to viewers is greater. Today, the general public witnesses the horrible toll taken by extensive damage to civil infrastructure, high numbers of civilian deaths, and widespread environmental damage wrought by large-scale conventional warfare. Consequently, it is hard for national leaders to sustain public support for such a war, while the promise of small-bore conflict with precise targeted killing makes for an attractive alternative to the same leaders. Particularly in a democracy, political leaders seek "to focus on as narrow a target as possible when considering how to enter a conflict."[14]

Another important factor promoting targeted killing is that it is more and more the case that individuals and not just states are true threats to security. The ability to obtain weapons of mass destruction (WMDs), particularly biological and chemical weapons, is within the reach of many well-financed and organized terrorists. Of course, there is no need to utilize WMDs to bring about great harm. No such weapons were part of the 9/11 attacks or other assaults on embassies, military compounds, and civilian groups by terror organizations. Regardless, the threat posed by a single leader or a relatively small group of terrorists has provided a rationale for targeted killing as an effective and low-cost way of protecting innocent people and maintaining national security.

And, finally, there is also the increased ability to engage in targeted killing as a policy. As recently as Operation Desert Storm in 1991, the number of precision-guided munitions used by the United States was below 8 percent. In 2003, in the second Iraq war, the number rose to 68 percent. In subsequent years, fighting in Iraq and Afghanistan, the U.S. military has used nearly 100 percent precision-guided munitions. In sum, "while individuals pose a greater threat to America than ever before, the United States likewise has a greater ability than ever before to target individuals and eliminate them."[15] For the foreseeable future it is very likely that targeted killing will be a policy used by the United States as well as other nations, particularly in asymmetric conflicts, that is, those conflicts where there are huge disparities between the military power, legal status, or strategies of the combatants. It is imperative, therefore, that there be an open and sustained debate about the wisdom and legitimacy of such a practice.

One aspect of that debate is the legal analysis of targeted killing. Acts of targeted killing in the context of armed conflict are clearly permissible under U.S. and international law. It has long been recognized that snipers may move about the front lines during a battle in order to kill an enemy military leader. That is one form of targeted killing. It is another matter, however, if the sniper's target is a political leader with no role in the enemy's chain of command. As noted previously, legitimate targeted killing is not the same as assassination.

Nor is it unarguably clear what counts as armed conflict to be governed by the laws of war where lethal force can be employed more broadly than in other environments. This is part of the debate concerning targeted killing in Pakistan, Somalia, and Yemen; these areas are not officially war zones, unlike targeted killing in the established conflict areas of Afghanistan and Iraq. The legal framework of armed conflict was designed with a model of interstate conflict in mind. It is less well suited to a model of armed conflict involving nonstate actors like terrorist organizations.

As will be discussed in chapters 3 and 4, arguments have been made that at least some of the traditional legal norms of armed conflict apply when dealing with groups like al-Qaida. Constraints like respect for state sovereignty place conditions on where and when the United States might target someone. Further, the laws of war require observance of norms like proportionality and discrimination that limit the who, when, and how of attacking targets. Taking such norms into account, the U.S. policy remains legally permissible, according to supporters.[16]

On the other hand, if the conditions of armed conflict do not pertain, then any U.S. administration is bound by the Constitution and international human rights law. Under these stricter constraints the government may only engage in lethal action after due process is followed in determining the target, or when targeted killing would be an act of last resort in order to respond to an imminent threat of deadly harm.[17]

One of the challenges to resolving the debate has been the lack of transparency on the part of the Bush and Obama administrations in presenting the government's view of the legal and moral grounds for the policy of targeted killing, particularly in Pakistan, Somalia, and Yemen. If the official policy were acknowledged, explained, and defended, then both supporters and opponents of the government's actions could argue specifics. Instead, we have both sides discussing a policy that is known only in general terms.

Signature Strikes

One of the most controversial types of targeted killing is the activity called "signature strikes" or, more recently, "terrorist attack disruption strikes." These are lethal attacks against a target defined as much by demography as by other evidence. In the lexicon of counterinsurgency a military-age male (MAM) is a category that extends to all men who are of fighting age, usually ranging from fifteen to seventy. In early 2008, George Bush approved the practice of attacking convoys of vehicles, even without positive identification of the identities of the people beyond their being MAMs, if the occupants appeared to be al-Qaida or Taliban fighters on the move, and when the risk of casualties beyond the convoy participants was low.

Due to the lack of transparency on the part of both the Bush and Obama administrations regarding the government's policy, there are not a lot of specifics about signature strikes. There are some facts that have come out due to leaks, on the ground research in the Middle East region, and occasional background briefings. In a strict sense, signature strikes do not really function as targeted killings since the specific identities of the targets are not known. Signature strikes are approved on the basis of behavior that suggests the individuals are associated with terror networks. For example, the CIA has engaged in "staggered drone strikes" or "double-tap" strikes, using a second attack to kill rescuers who arrive at the scene of the initial attack upon the first victims, the presumption being that it is fellow jihadists who would come to the rescue. There have also been targeted killings based on the presence of MAMs in areas where terrorists are known to be present.

The American policy of targeted killing poses a number of questions that will be addressed in chapters 4 and 5. Targeted killing underscores the difficulty of categorizing the actors and actions involved in contemporary armed conflict. Are the targets of targeted killing to be viewed as ordinary soldiers, illegal combatants, or civilian criminals? Is the motivation of targeted killing retribution, deterrence, interdiction, or preemption? Are targeted killings acts of legitimate self-defense or morally dubious executions? How are targets selected for targeted killing in the strict sense? For signature strikes? What are the ethical and legal bases for a policy of targeted killing outside declared battlefield areas? What is the review process for approving targeted killings of American citizens? What constraints are in place with regard to the exercise of presidential power? All these concerns, among others, require comment in any ethical assessment of targeted killing.

The current practice of using armed drone strikes to kill individuals identified as terrorist threats is the most commonly cited example of targeted killing. Before concluding this chapter it will be helpful, therefore, to provide a bit of background concerning drones and their use in America's counterterrorism strategy.

DRONES: THEIR NATURE AND USE

While the more technical term is unmanned or unoccupied aerial vehicles (UAVs), and the air force prefers remotely piloted aircraft (RPAs), the colloquial name of "drones" is widely used. In the 1970s and 1980s a branch of the Department of Defense called the Defense Advanced Research Projects Agency (DARPA) made early progress in the development of drones. This was still the era of the cold war and the original aim of DARPA was to fashion drones for surveillance purposes in the ongoing superpower rivalry.

In the mid-1990s there were efforts directed to arming drones in order to attack hard to reach targets. According to a leading researcher on drones, the interest in armed drones grew from the aim of killing Osama bin Laden after the deadly bombings of the U.S. embassies in Tanzania and Kenya.[18] However, armed drones were not ready at that time, which is why President Bill Clinton used cruise missiles in the 1998 attack on the al-Qaida training camps in Afghanistan and Sudan. "The first known killing by armed drones occurred in November, 2001, when a Predator targeted Mohammed Ater, a top al-Qaida military commander, in Afghanistan."[19] This was during George Bush's presidency.

At the time of the 9/11 attacks, the United States had roughly fifty drones; it now has thousands. The exact number is difficult to determine since the army and navy as well as the air force have drones. One educated guess puts the total number well above eight thousand. The vast majority of drones are used for surveillance. Of the total number, approximately three to four hundred drones are armed. The most common armed drones are the MQ-1 Predator and MQ-9 Reaper. It is not their weaponry that is notable about drones. They carry missiles that are commonly used by other military launchers and even the largest drones are not heavily armed. The most common missile on board is a Hellfire missile adapted from the army, which used it on helicopters to attack tanks and other armored vehicles. The air force adapted that missile to be more effective against personnel in an open setting. Drones are not fast: they move at speeds less than one hundred miles an hour; also, they fly low and are noisy.

What makes drones notable is "their ability to see and think."[20] Their navigational systems can be programmed so that drones are able to fly themselves from takeoff to landing. They are equipped with powerful visual sensors and video technology that permit surveillance in the dark and through clouds. Because they can fly themselves, their operators can focus on using that surveillance technology without distraction.[21]

Without doubt, drones are of great benefit to the counterterrorism effort. They have distinct advantages over manned aircraft, cruise missiles, and Special Operations attacks. First, unlike manned aircraft where refueling and crew fatigue limit flight time, drones permit sustained observation of potential targets for long periods of time. The exact duration of a flight is not public information but it is known to be longer than twenty-four hours for some models. And no pilot or ground observers are at risk during that time.

Second, unlike cruise missiles, drones are almost instantaneous in response time. When Clinton ordered the cruise missile attack on the suspected location of Osama bin Laden, the cruise missiles were targeted at a projected location for where he would be in four to six hours. What the military calls the cycle of "find-fix-finish" is reduced to seconds in the case of drones.[22] In addition, drone missiles can be diverted at the very last minute.

Third, drones are cost-effective when compared to manned aircraft. Drones have a greater propensity to mishaps than conventional aircraft but their significantly lower production costs still make drones more cost-effective.[23] The main reasons for drone crashes are bad weather, human error by operators, and disruption in communication links.[24]

Finally, drones do not require American troops to be placed in harm's way and, despite the protests over their use in places like Pakistan, they are a less dramatic violation of a nation's claim of sovereignty than an armed force invading on the ground.

Drones are launched from bases in Afghanistan, Pakistan, and other locales near where they are used.[25] They are piloted remotely by operators working at places such as Holliman Air Force Base in New Mexico and Nellis AFB in Nevada. The drones employed by the CIA are controlled by operators near Langley, Virginia. Remote control is not equivalent to robotic.[26] There are about 1,300 pilots trained to operate the drones and the air force now trains more drone pilots than bomber and fighter pilots annually. Even so, the flight shifts are frequent and long compared to manned aircraft and the demand for more drone flights is growing. Reportedly, many of the first wave of drone pilots are considering departing the air force due to the work conditions.[27]

REMOTE KILLING

One popular misconception about those piloting the drones is that they are so removed from the battlefield that the experience of war is like playing a video game. In truth, recent studies suggest that drone operators suffer from war trauma like other combatants and those who pilot manned planes.[28] The reason for this is the nature of the intense surveillance that drone pilots do prior to attack. "No doubt, the distance between the human warfighter and the battlefield has never been longer, but the psychological proximity can be closer for drone pilots than for other military personnel."[29]

Another dimension of drone pilots' experience is that they linger over a target site and witness the damage that they do, whereas pilots of manned planes hasten to leave once they have fired their weapons. Allied pilots in World War II killed countless numbers of civilians but they rarely would have experienced the results of their bombing. Drone pilots use weapons that are far more accurate than World War II's aerial bombs, but the pilots more often than not see close up the accidental deaths they cause.[30]

Yet there is a sense of incongruity when the carnage of a drone attack is contrasted with an image of the pilot finishing a shift and calmly driving home to have dinner with family members. Consequently, a variety of critics cite concerns about using remotely piloted vehicles in the act of killing. "Anonymous murder from a safe distance"[31] and the "video-game mentality of the drone controllers"[32] are typical comments in this vein.

Despite the superficial similarities between playing video games and remote piloting of drones, the latter is serious work for operators as well as deadly for victims. Dismissing it as video-gaming does not convey the true nature of the experience. Still, those operating drones are able to walk away unhurt if a drone should fall from the sky and that is a major reason why the use of drones is popular with both the Obama administration and the American public. In one poll of U.S. citizens, 72 percent were in favor and only 22 percent opposed the use of drone attacks in combatting terrorists.[33]

New forms of weaponry are often accompanied by moral concerns if they alter the nature of armed conflict, and drones have captured the attention of the general public because of the possibility that they might be such transformative weapons. The just war tradition maintains that war is a human activity subject to governance by moral norms. War cannot be removed from the realm of morality and still be just. So whether it be mounted cavalry or crossbows, catapults or submarines, nuclear bombs or attack drones, there will be new questions and debates surrounding the utilization of novel means of causing death—as well there should be.

Another issue raised by the "remoteness" of drone killing has been the suggestion that there is a lack of valor when one of the combatants, the drone operator, is at no real risk in the armed conflict.[34] The problem with this complaint is that one might have said the same thing about an archer in the Middle Ages firing from within a castle at a combatant on the ground outside, or a sniper shooting a sentry from hundreds of yards away, or a naval missile launcher seated at a console on a ship hundreds of miles from the field of battle. The issue of long-distance killing has been around for centuries and drones do not add much new to the topic.

There are other issues raised about remoteness, however, that merit reflection for defenders of drone killing. Is it possible that drones will subtly affect the way in which the military determines whether a target can be captured or killed by means that might better avoid civilian deaths? If the safety of the drone pilot becomes the standard by which one compares whether military personnel are put at risk, then we may wind up inverting the just war tradition. For one clear standard of that tradition is that soldiers must be willing to bear a measure of risk in order to avoid civilian casualties. That suggests to me that we ought not use drones to save American military lives if that only exacerbates the risk that falls upon foreign civilians.[35]

LEGAL, POLICY, AND MORAL CONCERNS

Although the United States generally avoids explicitly discussing that it follows a policy of targeted killing, it is evident from unclassified documents, official statements, and our government's actions that when the capture of a known terrorist is considered unfeasible the American government will use the Central Intelligence Agency or the U.S. military to kill the targeted individual.[36]

Many issues and questions arise as a result of this government policy. One set of questions is predominantly legal. Perhaps the basic issue in the debate is whether targeted killing is simply extrajudicial execution, prohibited by international and domestic law, since terrorists are civilians. Terrorists are criminals, not combatants, it is claimed, and should be captured and arrested using ordinary law enforcement measures and then prosecuted and punished according to the procedures of the criminal justice system. The other side of the debate proposes that terrorists are combatants in an armed conflict and may be legitimately targeted for killing according to the laws of warfare.

The UN Special Rapporteur believes that, "Outside the context of armed conflict, the use of drones for targeted killing is almost never likely to be legal."[37] However, as one commentator has correctly observed, "The trick, of course, is how we define 'armed conflict' in an age of non-state-affiliated terrorist and insurgent groups operating from places where the writ of a central government does not extend."[38]

The complicating factor is that international terrorism confounds much of the standard categories of international law. The premise of the international law on warfare is that two states engage in conflict, but the asymmetric war of counterterrorism involves nonstate actors using violent force against a state. Does counterterrorism demand a different paradigm than the binary model of it being either conventional warfare or standard police work?

Domestic U.S. law prohibits assassination by the military except in times of war. The Authorization for the Use of Military Force passed after 9/11 empowers the president to "use all necessary and appropriate force . . . in order to prevent any future acts of international terrorism against the United States." That would legitimate targeted killing by the American military against known terrorists, but it leaves unclear the actions of CIA personnel who are noncombatants according to the laws of war. Laws regarding congressional oversight of the CIA would also have to be examined to determine if targeted killings by the CIA have been in accord with the established regulatory regime.

There are also policy questions surrounding targeted killing. Advocates of targeted killing in the struggle against terrorists pose a simple question. Suppose targeted killing is banned as a tactic and suppose that in a number of cases arrest is impractical due to the degree of difficulty and amount of risk to the lives of others. Does that mean that some terrorists should be left free to continue to plot future attacks? Because that option seems undesirable to many, targeted killing is proposed as a defensible measure of last resort. Yet even if one grants that targeted killing may be appropriate in some narrowly circumscribed cases, there are still questions: who decides upon a target, by what criteria, what standard of evidence is necessary, what review procedures are in place, what procedure for holding decision makers accountable for errors is in place? The lack of transparency and public accountability for present government policy on targeted killing is a major area of concern.

Even if targeted killings are lawful by international and domestic standards, and even if there is a policy for targeted killing that is appropriate to a democracy, the question about its morality remains. And if some use of targeted killing is morally defensible, can there be immoral overuse? Might a person consider targeted killing a legitimate tactic in the fight against international terrorists while finding the tactic of signature strikes to be morally objectionable? Is there a place for targeted killing in a theory of just warfare? Must norms such as protection of innocent civilians and last resort be applicable? Is targeted killing preventive in nature, essentially defensive, or can it be used as punishment for terrorist acts already committed, a form of retributive justice?

The questions posed above make it clear that much of what we think we are discussing when talking about drones is really a conversation about targeted killing. The real issue is not drones, but the killing of militant terrorists or even suspect terrorists determined by unknown criteria in secret deliberations, with no hard data about the cost in innocent lives.[39]

Yet there are particular concerns about the use of armed drones as a specific mode of targeted killing; perhaps none more important than the issue of precedents. At present the United States is the dominant user of armed drones. But that will change. There are now more than fifty nations developing surveillance drones, and their military use will grow in time. The United States is in the position of setting the precedent for drone use and we ought to establish norms that we would wish others, including our rivals, to follow. For example, when defining the battlefield, what is to count as a combat zone in a future with thousands of drones in the air? Do we wish to live in a world where drones can attack anywhere—an urban park, a country lane, a suburban backyard, a fishing boat on a lake? Will everyplace be a potential battlefield where an attack can occur?

Another precedent to consider is the definition of who is a terrorist. Anyone who threatens a nation's security? That might be an investigative journalist or political dissident in the eyes of government leaders in some countries. A secretive process such as the United States has adopted in determining the targets of drone strikes establishes a precedent that we may regret once other nations have the capability to launch similar strikes at those individuals they deem to be legitimate targets on the basis of their national security.

The question of overreliance upon drones is another issue. "Since 9/11, over 95% of all non-battlefield targeted killings have been conducted by drones."[40] Drones have been especially effective in killing top al-Qaida leaders. Of the two dozen HVTs in the terrorist organization who have been killed, Osama bin Laden is the only one not to die as a result of a drone attack.[41] However, due to the effectiveness of the drone campaign there now appears to be a loosening of the criteria for targeted killing. Two scholars who have studied the targets of drone attacks have concluded that we are no longer killing HVTs but militant operatives of no particular significance. "On average, only one out of every seven U.S. drone attacks in Pakistan kills a militant leader. The majority of those killed in such strikes are not important insurgent commanders but rather low-level fighters."[42]

Drones, because they strike with impunity, suddenly, and almost anywhere, appear to have a singular ability to terrorize not only legitimate targets but people in general within a region under surveillance. Drone strikes also anger those concerned with border sovereignty. And because of the secrecy of the policy, there is also a public relations dilemma whereby the rationales for the strikes are not provided or their occurrence even acknowledged. This allows terrorists and militants to tell their version of who the victims were and what happened to them. As a result there has been a significant rise in antagonism toward the United States, with the consequence of less cooperation in intelligence gathering, as well as facilitating the recruitment of new members for terrorist networks.

Greater clarity about targeted killing and the use of armed drones in carrying out targeted killings is needed. Any moral assessment of drones is made more difficult if questions such as those noted above remain unanswered. In order to construct such a context I will examine three sources of discussion on the ethics of targeted killing. In the next chapter the wisdom within the Christian tradition as well as Judaism and the classical world of Greece and Rome will be consulted, and then in the two succeeding chapters I will present a lively debate among Israeli authors regarding targeted killing during the second Intifada, and the contemporary debate in the United States around our antiterrorist activities. Using the insights gleaned from this material I will in the fifth and final chapter assess the morality of the American use of drones as a means of targeted killing.

2

THE DISTANT CONTEXTS OF THE DEBATE

The practice of targeted killing has long been employed and debated among peoples of various places and times. Throughout Western history there have been arguments about the morality of assassination, tyrannicide, and other forms of killing aimed at specific individuals. In most circumstances the idea of targeted killing has been seen to violate the moral standards that support the protection of human life. Yet moral traditions have also found exceptional circumstances that have led to approval of targeted killing in particular cases.

In this chapter we will examine the distant context for a discussion of targeted killing. This distant context includes several traditions that have influenced thinking on the topic of targeted killing: classical Greek and Roman thought, ancient Judaism, and later Christian reflection. Western philosophical and legal writings have also contributed insight on the various forms of targeted killing.

TARGETED KILLING IN THE CLASSICAL WORLD

Perhaps the most discussed form of targeted killing throughout history has been tyrannicide. This specific form of targeted killing will be the focus for much of what follows. The historian Franklin Ford has written,

"For at least two and a half millennia it has constituted in the eyes of philosophers the only respectable link between ethics and political violence."[1] It was the discussion of tyranny in Aristotle's *Politics* that established the framework for much of what followed in the West. In accord with Plato, Aristotle maintained that whenever an entity contains a rational element it is proper for the rational part to rule over the nonrational. People differ in their capacity for rationality and, therefore, different modes of rule or governance are more or less suitable for different cases. A young child has a rational capacity that is incomplete and so it is appropriate for a father to rule over a child. Such paternal governance is inappropriate when the situation is of two adults with equal rationality.

For Aristotle despotic rule is illustrated in the master–slave relationship. Such rule can be justifiable because those who are "naturally" slaves lack the ability to be deliberative and are in need of a master to direct them.[2] Despotic rule is for the sake of the master, not the slave. When people have equal or similar rational ability, however, rule is to be for the sake of the ruled.[3] When there is proper rule by one it is monarchy, where the king rules for the good of all citizens. Political rule is a service that citizens provide for one another. It is aimed at the common good. A tyrant is a monarch who uses power not for the good of all citizens but for personal benefit. To Aristotle, political rule is perverted or defective when it is for the advantage of the ruler since this ignores the duty of political leadership to serve the common good of all citizens of the state.[4]

Tyranny, therefore, should be corrected; but the killing of the tyrant was not always the permissible path to restoring good political order. Aristotle's treatment in Book Five of the *Politics* entailed a "case study" approach that discussed a variety of examples of, and an array of motives for, tyrannicide in ancient Greece. Tyrannicide was possible if the ruler was a usurper or engaged in serious misrule. However, alternative measures for remedying the problem were preferable, if at all possible. Furthermore, if the tyrant was to be brought down, Aristotle assumed it was best done by elite representatives of the society—nobles, generals, religious leaders, and other figures of similar social standing. The idea was that such people, while not immune to self-interest narrowly understood, were likely to have some sense of a wider duty to the society as a whole. This assumption came to be called the *melior pars* (the better part) principle in subsequent theories of tyrannicide.

The true tyrant deserved death because he had made himself a person outside the law by his own capricious behavior. However, the assassin walked a thin line in trying to avoid a similar charge. Aristotle realized that, although necessary at times, resorting to tyrannicide opened a door to social disorder, even chaos. Thus, it was not a practice to be encouraged or made routine. If we follow the lead of the historian Franklin Ford and see tyrannicide as a particular species of assassination,[5] it may be claimed that ancient Greek thinkers like Aristotle frowned upon assassination in general but countenanced the possibility of some acts of tyrannicide. Nonetheless, there was concern that using tyrannicide as a defense against misrule ran the risk of "damaging the painfully acquired set of restraints lacking which *good* rule, too, could easily become impossible."[6]

Ancient Rome

Cicero, that great defender of the Republic, may have been the first Roman to defend tyrannicide, even by means of assassination. The assassination of Caesar overshadowed much of Cicero's writing of *De Officiis* (On Duties). Cicero observed that there was a distinction between particular duties and general ones, "For often the occasion arises when something that is generally and customarily considered to be dishonorable is found not to be so."[7] The particular example he cites to make this point about a duty in special circumstances is the killing of Caesar. His defense of the killing of Caesar became one of the most commonly cited precedents by later writers who took up the question. Cicero is clear that he viewed Caesar's death as tyrannicide and he repeats that assertion in several places in the text.[8] His only expressed lament is not over the death of Caesar but the fact that his death did not lead to the restoration of the Republic.

Caesar was not only elected consul but was also given the powers of dictator. This was a special office by which an individual was put at the head of the Republic and vested with extraordinary power. Usually dictators served for six months and acted with the consent of the Senate. Dictators were appointed by the consuls on the occasion of what we today might call national emergency. In Caesar's case it was civil war. For Cicero the great threat Caesar posed to the Republic, which was already in decline, was that Caesar was in his sixth year as consul and fifth year as dictator. This trend of greater power accruing to Caesar, who continued to hold one office that should have rotated and another that ought to have been temporary, threatened the very existence of the Republic. Though Caesar was not especially brutal or capricious in his rule, that was not the point for Cicero. Rather, it was the fear that "[w]ith the frequent and orderly rotation of elective government once broken by a military and political genius, how could anyone save the Republic from eventual oblivion?"[9]

Although not one of the conspirators himself, Cicero's voice was the one heard in the Senate calling for clemency for the assassins. He hoped to see a restoration of the normal workings of the Republic and an end to the rule by "strong men" who subverted the aristocratic and democratic roles of the Senate and the Assembly. It was not to be, however, as Cicero was slain less than two years later when the Second Triumvirate led by Mark Antony ordered his death.[10]

During the subsequent age of the empire there were abundant instances of assassination, including many that were driven more by palace intrigue and personal ambition than what might be justified by appeal to some theory of principled tyrannicide. In his history of political homicide, Franklin Ford suggests that the death of four Roman emperors might be cited as examples of "tyrannicides in keeping with the classical definition of usurpation or flagrant misrule, or both," which is not to deny there may have been other lesser motives involved as well.[11] On the whole, however, the number of assassinations that happened during the age of classical Rome leaves a clear sense that the vast majority of such killings had little to do with appeals to protection of the common good or resistance to unjust lethal aggression and were better explained by personal ambition or vengeance.

Curiously, the Roman practice of warfare against its external enemies seems to have been more reluctant concerning assassination than its internal politics might suggest. The Romans had a preference, perhaps out of a sense of honor but also due to confidence in their military prowess, for conquest on the battlefield over assassination of foreign enemies. Rome's military code prized victory through armed conflict that tested and rewarded valor while disdaining the use of deception and treachery. Here is an early source of what will be the later opposition to assassination based on the use of methods deemed dishonorable.

So a lesson from the classical world is that targeted killing in the form of assassination of a tyrant was sometimes permissible. Circumstances that might affect support for such killing included who committed the act (the *melior pars*, a private individual), the motive behind the act (defense of the common good, personal ambition, vengeance), and the nature of the tyrant (usurper, legitimate ruler).

TARGETED KILLING AND ANCIENT ISRAEL

During the intertestamental era, a period of approximately 450 years from the final quarter of the fifth century BC to the first quarter of the first century AD, Israel struggled against foreign powers to maintain independent rule and often suffered under governance by others. Persian, Greek, Egyptian, and Syrian armies successively imposed their rule upon the Jewish people. In 166 BC the Maccabean revolt took place that eventuated two years later in the defeat of Antiochus of Syria at Jerusalem, the rededication of the Temple to Yahweh after the desecration of pagan worship by Antiochus, and the pushing of Syrian forces out of Galilee in the north. The successors to the leadership of Judas Maccabeus came to be known as the Hasmonean dynasty, but they were not effective rulers.

In 64 BC one of the Hasmoneans appealed to Pompey to prop up the failed state and soon a Roman garrison was established at Jerusalem. The Romans, however, were less domineering than the earlier occupation forces and followed a policy of fairly lax oversight in cultural, especially religious, matters. As a result, the local Roman rulers found a number of Jews willing to accommodate to the imperial presence. Those more critical of Rome, while appealing to the legacy of Maccabeus, did not find sufficient support to mount a serious challenge to the Roman presence.

Those nonaccommodationists known as Zealots advocated violent resistance to the Roman presence in Palestine. They resisted the taxation that Rome imposed on its subject peoples. True theocrats, the Zealots wanted a society governed by Mosaic Law and they hated not only their Roman occupiers, but Jews who collaborated with the Romans. In place of the Roman Empire, which they saw as idolatrous, the Zealots wanted to establish a new Jewish state that could base its political order on Mosaic tenets. Lacking sufficient support among the general population to directly confront Rome, the Zealot movement went underground.

In time these Zealots were given a different name by the Romans, the *sicarii* or "dagger men" for their quiet but lethal attacks on Roman soldiers and other officials. The assassinations were not only employed against the Roman occupiers but also directed at those Jews deemed too cooperative with Rome.[12] The Zealots began a public revolt in AD 66 that led to disaster for the Jewish people as Rome forcefully quelled the uprising that ended with the mass suicide of the trapped revolutionaries at Masada. Most devastating was the complete destruction of the Jerusalem Temple, never again to be rebuilt.

Of course it was not the *sicarii* who were the first of the Hebrews to engage in assassination of despised political rulers. In the book of Judges there is the story that the Lord raised up Ehud to deliver the Israelites from the Moabite king Eglon, who had ruled over them for eighteen years. After offering the king the tribute from his people, Ehud stabbed the king using a dagger that had been kept hidden under his clothes. He fled before the body could be discovered. According to the narrative, Ehud then led a successful revolt against the Moabites and won the Israelite tribes their freedom.[13]

Following the story of Ehud there is also the tale of Deborah and Barak, she the prophetess and he the military leader who chose to attack the Canaanite foe. After the Israelite victory over the Canaanite army, the defeated general Sisera fled for his life. He was welcomed into the tent of one Jael, wife of a man that Sisera had reason to believe would protect him. Jael put the general at ease and encouraged him to rest while she would stand guard. However, while Sisera slept she killed him and later showed the corpse to Barak.[14] Later Deborah sings the praises of Jael as a blessed woman.[15]

The book of Judith, though set in the time of the Judges, is a fictional story most likely written sometime around 110 to 90 BC. It is a tale of an individual whose name simply means "Jewish woman." She represents a type, someone at the bottom of the social hierarchy of Israel, a childless widow. Yet she is portrayed as a model of faith, with more trust in God and courage against her foe than any of the males in the story. Judith uses her beauty and charm to draw close to Holofernes, the Assyrian general sent to punish the Jews for being disloyal vassals to Nebuchadnezzar. Seizing the opportunity to kill Holofernes while he lay intoxicated and sleeping, she uses the general's own sword to cut off his head and does it in the name of Yahweh who saves the people through unexpected means, such as this lowly woman. Biblical scholars see the book as a "reflection on the meaning of the yearly Passover observance."[16] It reminds the faithful Israelites that their God does not abandon them and will raise up individuals to save the people even if the deliverance comes in surprising ways.

Another story drawn from the era of the Judges tells the tale of Abimelech, one of the sons of Gideon born to his concubine. Gideon, a military leader of renown, left behind dozens of male heirs born to wives and concubines. Abimelech allies himself with the inhabitants of Shechem, an important town where his mother had kin. Making the case that he would be a better ruler over them than any of the other sons of Gideon because he was their kinsman, Abimelech gains the support of the Shechemites. Abimelech proceeds to systematically kill his fraternal rivals after hiring a group of thugs to do the work. He then proclaims himself king over the people and rules for several years before encountering a rebellion due to his misrule. During the siege of a city held by his opponents, Abimelech is attacked by a woman who hurls a stone and fractures his skull. As he lies dying, Abimelech orders one of his own men to hasten his death with a sword lest it be said that he died at the hands of a woman.[17]

These stories from the Book of Judges, as well as the tale of Judith situated in the era of the Judges, are set in the period between the conquest of Canaan and the establishment of the monarchy. Scholars believe the stories were independent of each other, rooted in tales of heroic military figures who led one or another of the tribes that identified with Yahwistic religion. Later editors redacted the collected stories and presented them as revealing a consistent religious message: because of infidelity the Israelite peoples risk the loss of the land that was promised to them and are ruled by enemies, but when they return in obedience to the covenant with Yahweh a deliverer is sent to free them from oppression.

The cycle of sin-punishment-repentance-deliverance is repeated again and again as generation after generation must learn the same hard lesson. Yet although God punishes the people for their infidelity, Yahweh never totally abandons the people but hears their cries for help and then comes to their aid. The Judges are portrayed in the Bible not as local tribal leaders, which they were, but as heads of a unified Israel that only came later with the establishment of the monarchy.

The incidents related above hardly reflect mature ethical reflection about targeted killing. Rather, the ethical concerns are all subjugated to the theological concern of the authors of what scholars call the Deuteronomist history. The message is that things go wrong when the Israelites break faith with Yahweh. Despite divine anger with their sinfulness, however, Yahweh consistently shows divine compassion when the people chosen to share in the covenant repent and return to observance of the teachings of the covenant. In order to bring about that compassionate deliverance from suffering, Yahweh will inspire sometimes unlikely figures to restore Israel's life. The theological message of divine activity may be reassuring to believers, but the ethical implications of claiming divine sanction for assassination and tyrannicide led to later difficulties, as we shall see.

The Rise of the Monarchy

It would be difficult to describe the development of the Israelite monarchy without delving into the various targeted killings that happened at the initial stages of the monarchy and continued through the generations of royalty afterward. The books of Samuel and Kings contain numerous incidents of targeted killing. Some of these are little more than vengeance killings for the earlier death of a blood relation (Joab stabbing Abner, 2 Sam 3:27) and some are little more than a calculated murder (David's plot against Uriah, 2 Sam 11:14–17 or Absalom's plot against Amnon, 2 Sam 13:27–30), but other killings appear to be the result of plots to seize power or defensive efforts to forestall such coups (death of Sheba, 2 Sam 20:14–22; Solomon's palace purge of Adonijah and Joab, 1 Kgs 2:12–35). While the narrator may describe examples of the first two types of killing as misdeeds or sins, the storyteller usually passes over without ethical judgment the deaths due to political intrigue. Although there is a minor voice of dissent in the historical books, the dominant strand of the tradition sees the institution of the monarchy as in accord with Yahweh's wishes and does not condemn those killings employed to maintain the rule of Saul, David, and Solomon.

With the division into northern and southern kingdoms, Israel and Judah, there is no letup in the bloodletting. With Solomon's death the north revolted at once, while the south remained loyal to the house of David. The first king in the north, Jeroboam, was a military leader who introduced foreign elements to Yahwistic religion and encountered prophetic opposition as a result. When his son, Nadab, took the throne, he was assassinated within two years by Baasha, another military leader. In accord with earlier prophetic judgments, Baasha slaughtered the entire family of Jeroboam. The text makes clear that this happened because Jeroboam and Nadab both angered Yahweh by their infidelity (1 Kgs 15:25–30). Baasha's family line, however, suffered a similar fate when his son, Elah, was killed by yet another military coup. The leader, Zimri, a lesser military figure, was quickly overthrown by Omri, the general of the Israelite army (1 Kgs 16:15–19). Omri's son, Ahab, also ruled Israel, and then came Joram, son of Ahab.

At this point the formidable presences of the prophets Elijah and Elisha enter the story. Ahab had married the foreigner Jezebel, who introduced the cult of the goddess Astarte and the great pagan god Baal. During her husband's reign Jezebel had the king's support in promoting these rival religious deities against the religion of Yahweh. Jezebel continued to have great influence as the queen mother once Joram succeeded to the throne. Prophetic opposition to Jezebel was fierce and by extension to the family line of Omri that provided two kings, Ahab and Joram, husband and son, respectively, who were supportive of Jezebel.

During Joram's reign the prophet Elisha encouraged the military commander Jehu to lead a rebellion against Joram that resulted in the death of Joram by an arrow that Jehu fired into Joram's back as he fled. This was just the initial act of violence as Jehu went on to see to the deaths of the queen mother Jezebel, dozens of Joram's family, the priests and worshipers of Baal in the northern kingdom, as well as the king of Judah and his kinsmen who were allied with Joram at the time—all done, presumably, with the support of Elisha. The story portrays all these killings as fulfillment of prophetic warnings about the fate of those who depart from the covenant fidelity to Yahweh (2 Kgs 9–10).

In general, the political intrigue due to tribal rivalries and warlords was more frequent and bloody in the northern kingdom of Israel than in Judah in the south. Yet assassinations and military coups were not unknown in the south: witness the deaths of the usurper queen Athaliah (2 Kgs 11:1–16) and the assassination of King Joash by disgruntled military (2 Kgs 12).

The united monarchy of Saul, David, and Solomon, along with the divided monarchies of northern and southern kingdoms, presided over centuries of violence, brought on by misrule, personal ambition, religious intolerance, and political calculations. The biblical text records some of the killing as morally offensive and sinful but not all of it. There are many killings sanctioned by religious figures that are portrayed as being in accord with the will of Yahweh.

It is this religious dimension to many of the targeted killings one finds in the Old Testament that is notable. What is evident is the strong belief in the role of a transcendent source of judgment that stands over even a king. No monarch was ever seen from the Hebrew perspective to be above the law of God. In many ways the sordid tales of killing convey the fundamental claim that those who do evil, those who offend God by abusing their duties as king, will come to a tragic end. No one is beyond God's judgment; not even a king is immune to divine punishment. That conviction of the ancient Israelites, along with the violent history of the monarchies, will shape the outlook of Christians in later centuries when the questions of tyrannicide and assassination arise.

TYRANNICIDE IN THE CHRISTIAN TRADITION

There is very little in the actual texts of the New Testament that might be used to support the idea of tyrannicide. The preaching and teaching of Jesus is dominated by the theme of the reign of God and that message was not to be confused in any way with the hopes of those Zealots living at the same time as Jesus.[18]

What one does find in the New Testament texts is guidance for those disciples living after the Jesus of history who must live under the political authority of the Roman Empire. In Paul's letter to the Romans (13:1–7) and the first letter of Peter (2:13–18) there are exhortations to live peaceably with political authority even when rulers are less than just in their governance. The later author of Revelation has witnessed the persecution of Christians by Roman emperors and while these rulers are identified as being in league with Satan and opposed to the Gospel, the Christian opposition is verbal with no call to rebellion or violence in the face of injustice. Indeed, the writer acknowledges that disciples will be placed in captivity and some will be slain by the sword and yet the response should not be an assault against the empire, but a call to live "the faithful endurance of the holy ones" (Rev 13:10).

Patristic era writing on the topic of targeted killing is scant in the Latin West, although there are a few instances of Eastern Greek authors discussing the topic, with some expressing openness to tyrannicide for religious reasons. The biblical examples of Ehud and Judith were cited by

Greek fathers and they were also aware of the ideas of classical writers like Aristotle. John Chrysostom interpreted Paul's teaching in Romans to mean that "the power of the office was ordained by God, but not necessarily the ruler."[19] Another influential text, written by the historian Sozomen, was an account of the death of the emperor Julian the Apostate (d. 363). Sozomen maintained the killer was a Christian and added, "Greeks and all men unto this day have praised tyrannicides for exposing themselves to death in the cause of liberty. . . . Still less is he deserving of blame, who for the sake of God and of religion, performed so bold a deed."[20] So the patristic record is neither completely silent nor united in disapproval of tyrannicide.

In the West, however, Augustine was an opponent of such killing, believing that unjust rulers were using their power, even if unwittingly, according to God's designs. For the Latin fathers, God established rulers in some cases to protect and serve, while in other cases to chasten and punish.[21] Nonetheless, those in authority were given their power by God and it was not for any subject to boldly alter that divine plan. Because of Augustine's long shadow, discussion of tyrannicide among Christians was stifled for centuries within the Roman Church.

It was not until the twelfth century that the topic arose again.[22] John of Salisbury was a disciple of Thomas Becket and an eyewitness to the events surrounding Becket's martyrdom. As one might expect from a close colleague of the bishop, John was critical of Henry II, who was implicated in Becket's murder, and considered the king a tyrant. John also criticized the emperor Frederick Barbarossa for tyrannical behavior. Trained in political philosophy, John was influenced by Cicero, and like his Roman predecessor approved of some tyrannicide, stating that it could be both licit and morally just. In John's mind, a king who ruled rightly was indeed a reflection of God's justice and authority, but a tyrant reflected the image of the devil's power, not God's. As Ford asks, "Could a pious author have defined the polarity in more emphatic terms?"[23] The viewpoint John espoused did not have great influence upon his contemporaries, but his ideas did influence later writers due to being cited by Grotius in the *Laws of War*.[24]

Thomas Aquinas

More influential was the approach of Thomas Aquinas, who treated the question of tyrannicide in several places. In his *Commentary on the Sentences* Aquinas demonstrates he is aware of Cicero's view but the nonresistance texts of Romans 13:2 and 1 Peter 2:13 weigh more heavily in his thinking. If the tyrant demands that one do something that is manifestly unjust and against conscience, a person not only has no obligation to obey, but has a duty not to obey. Nonobedience does not lead to the act of tyrannicide, however, but rather a willingness to imitate "the case of the holy martyrs who suffered death rather than obey the ungodly commands of tyrants."[25]

Aquinas does not take up the question in his most famous work, the *Summa Theologiae,* but he does touch upon a related matter in Book II, Part II where he discusses the question of whether one who is condemned to death may resist either through flight or force. Aquinas distinguishes between those justly condemned and those condemned unjustly. Regarding the former Aquinas denies the possibility of legitimate resistance, but regarding the latter he likens unjust condemnation to the violence of robbers and declares, "even as it is lawful to resist robbers, so is it lawful, in a like case, to resist wicked princes."[26]

Does "resistance" equate to individuals taking it upon themselves to kill an evildoer? Here Johnstone cautions against reading Aquinas as approving tyrannicide. If one looks at an earlier question in the same section, Aquinas asks about whether it is lawful to kill a sinner. He answers no, since it is only licit to kill an evildoer if it is done for the good of the entire community. "The care of the whole community is committed to the prince having public authority. Therefore, it is lawful only for the prince to kill malefactors; it is not allowed to private persons."[27]

In *De regimine principum* (On the Rule of Princes) Aquinas takes up the question again in a more extensive way. He advises that the best path is to avoid letting rulers become tyrants. Faced with the fact of unjust rule, however, he argues that a tyrant may be deposed, but he is more circumspect on the question of killing the tyrant. Johnstone, in keeping with the view expressed above about killing a sinner, concludes that Aquinas did not believe a person of inferior status should take a tyrant's life. In addition to that principled opposition, Aquinas also held a prudential opposition on the ground that things may likely get worse rather than better after tyrannicide.

If a person of inferior status is not permitted to commit tyrannicide, might a superior kill a tyrant? To my knowledge Aquinas nowhere explicitly acknowledges this, though one may infer from his position on capital punishment of wrongdoers that a superior, an emperor, might impose such a penalty upon a tyrant if necessary.

To sum up the position of Aquinas we may cite Johnstone, who makes four points:

1. If a tyrant holds power legitimately then a private individual may not take the tyrant's life.
2. If there is a person with superior authority then that person may depose a tyrant.
3. If no such superior authority exists, then it is for those persons who can reasonably claim to represent the people as a whole to deal with the matter (the *melior pars*).
4. In the cases of points 2 and 3 it appears to be the view of Aquinas that the tyrant could be killed if there is no other way to safeguard the common good.

Nowhere, however, does Aquinas explicitly commend the killing of a tyrant.[28]

Developments after Aquinas

A precedent in opposition to tyrannicide, cited by many later commentators, was the condemnation of the view of Jean Petit by the Council of Constance. Jean was a teacher in Paris who defended the killing of the Duke of Orleans in 1407 on orders from the Duke of Burgundy. The council's condemnation, however, was of Petit's blunt and unnuanced position that anyone could kill a tyrant by any means without resort to any legal process. Thus it could be argued that a more limited and defined form of tyrannicide did not fall under the ban. As Ford demonstrates in his historical treatment of political killings, Petit's argument was more rhetorical than analytical. Yet he provided a handy foil for later writers who would express their disagreement with Petit's radical view and then appear moderate by proceeding to argue a more limited case for tyrannicide.

One significant outcome of Petit's defense of the killing and the later conciliar condemnation was the identification of assassination with treacherous methods, which seems to date from the conciliar decision. Ford suggests the opposition to use of such dishonorable means may be further traced to the moral residue of the knightly code of chivalry as well as the military code of ancient Rome.[29]

Despite the general reluctance to endorse tyrannicide in theory, the practice of tyrannicide and the broader violence of assassination continued, with some locales, like Italy in the Renaissance era, being particularly known for the practice. The Republic of Venice in the fifteenth century was notable for its abundant use of assassination as an element of its foreign policy. Indeed, the Venetian policy gave rise to "rent-an-assassin" businesses that would post fees in advance for killing various notables, including the pope.[30] A pope might not be just a victim in this business. In an infamous plot against Lorenzo de Medici and his brother Giuliano, the Archbishop of Pisa was a major conspirator while Sixtus IV knew of the plot and was reportedly deeply upset when it failed.[31]

The use of assassination was not limited to Italian city-states, as Spain was also a prime locale for assassination plots. The practice became even more widespread with the religious wars that followed the Protestant reformation. In England, Thomas More defended assassination as a legitimate tool of statecraft and, in a theme that will return in contemporary debates, as a morally preferable way to resolve disputes rather than going to war.[32] Philip II of Spain was a strong advocate of the assassination of Protestant leaders, plotting against both William of Orange and Elizabeth I. So prevalent did assassination become during the sixteenth century that most treatises within the nascent field of international law gave approval to the practice. It appears that the chief contribution of Christian faith during this time was not to moderate appeals to tyrannicide but to advance a new reason for it, namely, promotion of false religion, which was a charge used by both Protestant subjects against Catholic rulers and Catholic subjects against Protestant rulers.

Despite the practice of assassination becoming widespread, it did not necessarily follow that the theoretical underpinnings to approve or oppose the act had attained greater clarity. In his historical treatment Ford refers to the era of "Monarchomachs," literally a "fighter against monarchs." The term as used by historians was "to signify a believer in defiance of oppressive rule and, more specifically, one who tends to concentrate on the ruler's alleged offenses against a 'true' religion."[33] Because a heretical ruler was an outcast before God, there was no reason to maintain divine approval and protection of the ruler.

Although it was Lutheran theologians who initially developed a theory of resistance based on constitutional law arguments, Lutherans came to accept the compromise made within the Holy Roman Empire concerning the principle that the religion of the prince would be the religion of the people. Since many German princes followed Luther, German Lutherans found the compromise tolerable. This was also the case in Scandinavia. For Catholics it was only in Henry VIII's England and a few German and Swiss city-states where they experienced politically imposed religious repression so they, too, acquiesced to the principle. It was among the followers of John Calvin, who were victimized by rulers in France, Scotland, and the Dutch Netherlands, that the need to articulate a rationale for resistance was felt most keenly.[34]

Calvinism and Monarchomachs

The emergence of Calvinist monarchomachs was not due simply to geography. Calvin and his followers had great respect for the Old Testament and they naturally sought to integrate various biblical lessons about unfaithful monarchs along with the classical Greek and Roman insights about the danger of tyranny. Since Calvinists were drawn from the ranks of feudal nobility and the magistrates of large towns, they tended to endorse the various rights of feudal and bourgeois resistance to overbearing monarchs. When blended with the Old Testament teachings, the result was a strong ethos of opposition to ungodly kings. Theodore of Beza, Calvin's close ally in Geneva, spoke at a colloquy called by Charles IX, king of France, at which he advocated the idea of resistance when confronting misrule.[35]

Calvin himself held the standard view that Christians had a duty of obedience to proper political authorities. This was related to his doctrine of providence, for government was a sign of God's ongoing care for creation, establishing security, peace, and justice in a world that might otherwise break down into social chaos. Rebellion against government was equated with a loss of hope in the providential care of God, who was the founder of civil government.

True, a given ruler might be less than just, but the duty of obedience was not premised upon the virtue of the ruler but upon the divinely ordained office of temporal authority. As with some Old Testament prophets, a bad ruler was viewed as God's punishment upon a people for their sins. God's providence allowed for use of bad government to chasten and instruct a people in need of patience and humility. Calvin's conviction regarding divine providence being at work even when government was oppressive is evident in letters he wrote cautioning against those who too quickly moved to rebellion. He opposed the views of his follower John Knox who had written a denunciation of Mary, Queen of Scots, exhorting Protestant reformers to depose her.[36]

The lone exception Calvin granted in his opposition to rebellion was if a temporal ruler enforced a law or policy that directly contravened one's religious conscience. Aquinas and Luther also thought one might refuse to obey, as long as one was willing to suffer the penalty. Calvin went a bit further, however, with the implication that a believer might look upon the ruler in such a case as no longer a duly constituted authority. In a comment about the commandment to honor one's parents, Calvin discussed the case where parents encourage behavior contrary to God's will. "If they instigate us to any transgression of the law, we may justly consider them not as parents, but as strangers who attempt to seduce us from obedience to our real Father. The same observation is applicable to princes, lords, and superiors of every description."[37]

While seemingly a mild comment that hardly called for a rush to the barricades or launching a program of assassinations, what might follow from Calvin's observation is addressed in another famous passage from the *Institutes*:

> For though the correction of tyrannical domination is the vengeance of God, we are not, therefore, to conclude that it is committed to us who have received no other command than to obey and suffer. This observation I always apply to private persons. For if there be, in the present day, any magistrates appointed for the protection of the people and the moderation of the power of kings, such as were in ancient times . . . I am so far from prohibiting them, in the discharge of their duty, to oppose the violence or cruelty of kings, that I affirm that if they connive at kings in their oppression of the people, such forbearance involves the most nefarious perfidy, because they fraudulently betray the liberty of the people, of which they know that they have been appointed protectors by the ordination of God.[38]

This passage, endorsing the duty of duly appointed public officials to restrain and even resist a king, became a subject of much commentary. It is not all that distant from the viewpoint of Aquinas. Nonetheless, it is a significant text because this modest exception to a general prohibition of resistance to a king led to far broader claims by Calvin's disciples. John Knox in Scotland, Johannes Althusius in the Netherlands, and the influential author of the anonymous *Vindiciae, Contra Tyrannos* in France took Calvin's statement and developed it into a right of resistance not reserved only to political officials acting out of public duty, but into a general right of resistance to rulers who fell out of favor with the general population. This revised theory developed in two steps.

In Calvin's Geneva, where he was the most important civic leader as well as the undoubted spiritual leader in the city, talk of resistance to a temporal ruler had little resonance. The situation for Calvin's followers outside of Geneva was dramatically different. In places where the Calvinist interpretation of the Christian tradition had significant support among the population, there were Catholic monarchs willing to use state power to punish the reformers. It was in these regions where Calvinists altered their leader's teaching.

As one historian of political thought summarizes it, "Calvin's political theory was a somewhat unstable structure, not precisely because it was illogical but because it could readily become the prey of circumstances." Calvin taught the wrongfulness of resistance to constituted authority; he also taught the duty of the church to proclaim correct doctrine with the support of secular authority. "It was practically a foregone conclusion, therefore, that a Calvinist church, existing in a state whose rulers refused to admit the truth of its doctrine and to enforce its discipline, would drop the duty to obey and assert the right to resist."[39] At least, that was the likely outcome if there were little reason to hope the state's ruler might be converted. Such was the precise case in Scotland, the Netherlands, and France.

Step one in the development of the theory begins in Scotland. The Calvinist preacher John Knox found himself under a death sentence issued by the Catholic bishops with the agreement of a Catholic monarch. Yet Knox was popular among the public and had significant support among the lesser nobility. The choice was clear: accept the judgment of a king and church deemed in heresy or call for a change of leadership. Knox issued his call for resistance on the ground that the higher duty is not obedience to a monarch, but the duty to bring about religious reform.

With Knox there was an alteration of the ban against rebellion, yet the basis for the change was an appeal to religious duty. It was in France that step two would be taken, when the theoretical foundation for rebellion became not religious duty but the right of the people to rebel. The right was asserted because the monarch was viewed as answerable to the people from whom the royal power was derived.

Arguably, the most famous example of the argument for the right to rebel is contained in the document *Vindiciae, Contra Tyrannos* ("Vindication, Against Tyrants"), a work that has never been definitively ascribed to a particular author. It was representative of Huguenot thought that opposed the policies of French monarchs in the late sixteenth century. The text addressed four questions: Must subjects obey a prince in violation of God's law? Is it lawful to resist a prince who is destroying God's church, and by what manner of resistance? Is it permissible to resist a tyrant destroying the commonwealth? Should a monarch of one kingdom assist the rebellion in another kingdom where there is religious and political oppression? The answers to all four questions were developed from a mix of biblical theology, natural law philosophy, and Roman legal theory. The upshot was an impressive synthesis making a case against divine right theories of absolute monarchy.

With regard to the first question, God had entered into a covenant with the king, who was, in effect, a trustee of God's possession, the people. Such trusteeship required the king to rule rightly and failure to do so canceled the people's obligation to obey. Second, both king and people are, as a result of their covenant with God, duty bound to uphold and protect the church; if one of the parties should falter in this regard, the other party must fulfill the covenant obligation. Relying upon earlier medieval conciliarist thinking, and in accord with Calvin's teaching, the author did not vest private individuals with the authority to act in resistance against a legitimate ruler; rather, it was the official agents of the people—magistrates, council or parliament members, lesser nobles—who had the responsibility to act.

Concerning the third question, the author introduced a different form of covenant that directly placed ruler and people in relation to each other and not in relation to God. It is the people who are the party to charge their rulers with the obligation to secure their well-being. The people put themselves into the care of rulers and those who accept the obligations of rule must meet the demands that are established, or else be guilty of betraying their covenant partner. Borrowing from the biblical accounts of Hebrew monarchs, the king may be chosen by God but the people then must confirm the divine appointment. Finally, regarding the fourth question, the author asserts the unity of the church and suggests that each ruler has an obligation to defend true doctrine and practice throughout the church. No ruler can shirk that duty on the ground that the offense against the church is outside his or her realm.

The *Vindiciae* was not without its internal inconsistencies and twists of logic. And it presumed a situation of church unity, and of a popular majority in union against a monarch, that was not at all descriptive of the actual situation in France. Yet its argument served as a clear harbinger of the emerging theory of popular rights and the belief that a monarch might be resisted in the name of the people.

The upshot of the Calvinist tradition can be summarized in four points.

1. Calvin's doctrine of God's providential care led him to a general opposition to resort to tyrannicide. The sole exception he countenanced was when a ruler compelled a person to violate his religious conscience.
2. In discussing that exception Calvin appeared to question whether a ruler remained legitimate. He maintained that others within a state charged with care for the commonweal had a duty to depose such a ruler.
3. Followers of Calvin, writing in political situations that were more disadvantageous to Calvinists than Geneva, expanded that duty of public officials into a generalized right of violent resistance to rulers who lacked popular support. This was justified on the grounds that the higher duty is not obedience to a ruler but the promotion of correct religious teaching.
4. Finally, in the writing of Calvinist thinkers the appeal to religious duty morphed into a right to rebel when the people feel that a ruler violates the covenant by which the ruler serves as a trustee of the people who are God's possession.

The Jesuit Response

Roman Catholicism came more slowly to a discussion of tyrannicide during the Reformation era. In the eyes of Rome the entire Protestant Reformation was an exercise in sedition, and the reformers were guilty of transgressing against both Christian and civil authority. Jan Hus had been burned at the stake and Martin Luther might well have experienced the same were it not for the protection given by Frederick, the Elector of Saxony.[40] The popes of the era in their antagonistic behavior toward Protestant rulers may have encouraged the idea of tyrannicide for religious reasons, but there was not much done by way of theological or ethical justification.

It was only after a sufficient number of royal rulers had embraced Protestant beliefs that the Roman church sensed a threat real enough to reconsider the issue of tyrannicide. Two Spanish Jesuits, Juan de Mariana and Francisco Suarez, played important roles in the Catholic debate over tyrannicide. Mariana suggested that harm to religion was one of the hallmarks of a tyrant that served as a rationale for legitimating resistance. Tyrannicide was acceptable, and in the case of a usurper the killing could be done by anyone. For a legitimate but tyrannical ruler greater prudence must be exercised but, in the end, tyrannicide still could be permitted. Mariana's book, published in 1599, stirred a controversy at the time but came to be infamous after the assassination of Henry IV of France in 1610.

Although Henry had converted to Catholicism there remained lingering doubts about his Protestant sympathies. The saying attributed to Henry, that "Paris was worth a mass," is apocryphal, but is in the eyes of many historians a fair description of his attitude. His adoption of Catholicism was motivated by political ambition, not religious conviction.[41] Whatever his religious sensibility, Henry had been a popular ruler early in his reign and still held a measure of the public's goodwill when he was assassinated by a religious fanatic who claimed he was told by God to kill the king. The reaction to the assassination was revulsion and Mariana's book was seen as a contributory cause to the idea of assassination of a monarch for religious reasons. Mariana's work subsequently was condemned by the government in Paris. It also evoked reprisals against the Jesuits, and the Jesuits' Superior General issued a decree forbidding any Jesuit from teaching the idea that it is lawful for a person, under any pretext, to kill a civil ruler.

In the case of Suarez his political theory was worked out as part of a comprehensive theory of law. Suarez revised much of the medieval heritage of natural law and synthesized it so that it served as a precursor of constitutional and international law. He acknowledged that the papacy had no temporal authority, except over the Papal States in central Italy. Yet Suarez maintained the pope does have authority over all spiritual matters, and this implied a measure of indirect temporal authority insofar as temporal matters affect spiritual concerns.

Suarez argued that no king serves by divine right, if by that it is meant a king receives authority directly from God. Only the pope, as Vicar of Christ and spiritual head of the church, had authority directly from God. Temporal power, on the other hand, comes from the community of people who possess it, in order to attain the proper ends of social life. Secular authority had no direct mandate from God in the exercise of power; instead, temporal rulers receive their power as designates of the community. Temporal authority flows from the commitment to act on behalf of the people and in accord with the natural law. Therefore, no secular ruler can expect absolute obedience from the people since the ruler's authority ultimately is founded upon being the vicar of the people, acting on their behalf to promote the goods of social life that contribute to human well-being. Because the papacy has its spiritual authority directly from God it trumps secular authority whenever a spiritual good is at stake. So there are cases when a pope can depose a ruler: if, for example, the ruler is leading his subjects into heresy and suppressing the legitimate freedom of the church.

Suarez was steeped in the Thomistic approach and in most ways his views on monarchy were similar to Aquinas. He accepted the idea that when a legitimate ruler does wrong it is best for people to bear such injustice with patience and trust in God's final justice. Yet Suarez distinguished between the tyrant as legitimate ruler and the tyrant as a usurper. The tyrant as usurper wages a war against the people as members of a society, but also against each individual member. Therefore the usurper can be resisted by the people as a whole or by any individual.

Where Suarez differed from Aquinas was in his belief that heresy and a ruler's use of compulsion in a false cause were sure signs of tyranny even in legitimate rulers. The people as a collective may oppose legitimate rulers who fall into tyranny, although individuals may not attack a tyrant who is not a usurper. Private individuals may defend themselves, however, if directly attacked by the tyrant. In the latter case, although the individual does not have jurisdiction to kill the ruler, the act is done with the authority of God who, through natural law, gives to each person the power to engage in self-defense.[42] Although Suarez's work was published after the death of Henry IV it was "conceived and essentially completed prior to Henry's assassination."[43]

Just about the time that Suarez wrote on tyranny (1613) the attitude toward international or foreign assassination underwent a dramatic change, in part due to Henry's death, but also because of several other high-profile assassinations or attempted ones. It might be expected that the Thirty Years' War would have been a time of increase in assassinations, yet the historical evidence points to a significant decline from the preceding decades. For example, Emperor Ferdinand II and Philip IV of Spain refused to entertain the assassination of Gustav Adolf of Sweden, even as his Protestant armies won crucial battles against them. Eventually, when the religious wars declined, the sentiment against assassination grew even stronger until by the eighteenth century it was the widely prevailing viewpoint. Indeed, when Emmerich de Vattel wrote his treatise on international law in 1758 he described foreign assassination as "infamous and execrable."[44]

Alphonsus Liguori

Catholic moral theology in the eighteenth century developed a literary genre called "the manuals." These were summaries of moral teaching, presented by moral theologians for the instruction of priests and seminarians as they gave guidance and instruction to their people. Alphonsus Liguori was a leading author in this period whose manuals went through multiple revised editions. He was generally a moderate in his presentation of the church's teaching, avoiding the extremes of rigorism or laxism. In the case of tyrannicide, however, Liguori can be read as staking out one end of the Catholic debate in opposition to the Jesuits, particularly Mariana.

In a work written for pastors, *Homo Apostolicos*, published in 1759, Liguori argued that an individual may never kill a tyrant, even one who is a usurper. He goes so far as to oppose the appeal to legitimate self-defense in the case of a subject under attack by a prince, even though he accepts self-defense in private life. Liguori offers two rationales for this restriction. First, a prince is a "sacred" person whose death would cause great harm to a republic. Johnstone notes that Liguori was apparently a supporter of some version of divine right of kings, in stark contrast to the earlier medieval view passed on through Suarez.[45]

The political situation of the time was a second influence upon Liguori's stated position. He was writing during the period, noted above, that saw a decline in the number of assassinations and a general public opposition to such political killing. In fact, Liguori lived in Naples, where the king had come to power after a violent battle and with support from outsiders. Still, the Bourbon King Charles was accepted by the majority, though technically he could be considered a usurper. Liguori's opposition to any individual attacking a prince fit well with the circumstance in which he found himself.

Liguori's influence on the later Catholic tradition was substantial as subsequent authors of manuals in moral theology often developed their positions through commentary on his views. His thinking on tyrannicide established a normative position that was at the opposite end of the spectrum from that of Mariana and the monarchomachs. Even when later authors considered the possibility of a justified tyrannicide in principle, they often refrained from making it a practical option by raising the prudential concern about avoiding a greater harm. The prospects of civil war, social anarchy, or dynastic feud encouraged caution among moral theologians when discussing tyrannicide.

For example, one manual distinguished tyrants in act, those who are legitimate rulers but who abuse authority, from tyrants in title, that is, usurpers. The tyrant of the first type may not be killed by the private individual who does not have the authority to act in the name of the nation. The usurper, however, may be killed if he is in the role of a public enemy seeking to take possession of the title of ruler. However, once the usurper gains the title of ruler then the same prohibition against tyranny applies as with the first case.[46]

By way of summarizing what one finds in the theological tradition, it is necessary to acknowledge a degree of pluralism among theologians. While one strand of the tradition proposes that the justification for a lethal attack on a tyrant can be explained through the ethical framework of self-defense, the other strand argued an assault upon a ruler must be dealt with using a more juridical framework requiring proper jurisdiction on the part of those opposing the tyrant as well as due process to ascertain the rightness of the action. Other writers within the tradition were split on the question of tyrannicide, depending upon whether the tyrant was a usurper or a legitimate monarch engaged in misrule. Individual or collective self-defense might be allowed to justify killing a usurper, but the more juridical process was the norm for opposing a tyrant who was a legitimate ruler. And almost all authors worried about the danger that following the death of a tyrant even worse social calamity might be unleashed. It is clear, however, that tyrannicide as a form of targeted killing was judged permissible by many authors, Catholic and Protestant.

ASSASSINATION

Although it is the kind of targeted killing that has elicited the most moral commentary over the centuries, tyrannicide is but one form of targeted killing. Another type of targeted killing with a long history is assassination. "The Latin word *Assassinus* seems to have occurred for the first time in a European legal text in a decree of Innocent IV promulgated at the Council of Lyons in 1245."[47] The word was not unknown prior to the papal decree, as it originated as a term of derision aimed at a particular branch of Islam whose members were alleged to use hashish prior to engaging in lethal attacks on crusaders and Christian pilgrims in the Middle East.[48] Or so the legend goes.

While assassination came to be treated as a crime in canon law, carrying the penalty of excommunication, no link was developed between it and tyrannicide. Rather the word was associated with killing that was done for bad motives and by dishonorable means. Johnstone reports that despite the widespread practice throughout history of assassination, understood as killing done by treachery or underhandedness for a bad motive, there was not a great deal of attention given to it by moral theologians.[49] This is not surprising, however, if we understand that assassination was associated with bad will and dishonorable killing. Given that description, assassination was deemed wrong and not treated as a type of killing where the moral assessment was in debate. It was because tyrannicide was understood as possibly legitimate in some circumstances that much was written on it. Moralists like to discuss complex and open cases, not those deemed settled and closed.

If we turn to more modern times, during the Napoleonic Wars the British Foreign Secretary was approached about an assassination plot against Napoleon. Not only did he refuse to support the plan, but he had the potential assassin arrested and informed the French foreign minister of the plan.[50] When the U.S. Army adopted the Lieber Code in 1863 and many nations adopted the treaty of the 1907 Hague Conference, it was clear that assassination was now viewed with profound misgiving. That settled the matter, in principle, as far as international law has been concerned. Simply put, there were honorable and dishonorable ways to engage an enemy, and assassination was identified with the dishonorable methods.[51] However, terms used in the language of the Hague treaty were ambiguous and undefined and proved to be a source of debate for decades. The Geneva Conventions, signed after World War II, did not clarify the language either.

As is widely known, one of the triggers for the start of World War I was the assassination of Archduke Franz Ferdinand, the heir to the throne of the Austro-Hungarian Empire. A major reason why tensions grew into violent conflict was that the empire maintained the Serbian government was complicit in the 1914 act, and this was viewed as an outrage for a government to sponsor assassination. After the war, the Soviet Union under Lenin and then Stalin resorted to assassination often, although it was usually aimed at Russian dissidents living abroad, not foreign nationals, and there is little evidence that the policy was aimed against foreign leaders. In sum, by the twentieth century international assassination of a nation's leaders was widely treated as an act beyond the pale for a legitimate state.

Hitler's approval of the assassination of Dollfuss, the Austrian chancellor, was strongly condemned and viewed as a prime example of the Nazi disregard for international law. As for assassination plots against Hitler himself, the British explicitly rejected the idea until the final year of the war when it was considered as a way to bring the war to a close more quickly. The most well-known plots against Hitler originated with German nationals, not foreign governments, and might be considered failed attempts at tyrannicide.

During the Cold War, however, there were a number of assassinations. The Belgian government assisted native actors in the killing of Congolese Prime Minister Patrice Lumumba, who was viewed as being sympathetic to the Soviet Union. And later investigations revealed that the United States had earlier plotted to assassinate Lumumba. The CIA was also involved in the assassination of Mohammad Mosadegh of Iran in 1953, Jacobo Arbenz Guzman of Guatemala in 1954, Ngo Dinh Diem of South Vietnam in 1963, Salvador Allende of Chile in 1973, and in failed attempts aimed at Fidel Castro of Cuba.[52]

Public knowledge of these activities came to light during the investigative hearings held by both branches of the American Congress during the 1970s. There was much outrage at the revelations resulting in presidential action banning any U.S. employee from engaging in the plotting of or carrying out an assassination. It was Gerald Ford in 1976 who issued the first ban, and it has been reaffirmed by each president ever since.

This broad consensus on the wrongfulness of assassination has in recent decades been revisited. Due to the experience of modern terrorist activity there have been calls for treating the assassination of terrorists as a necessary and legitimate response by those states victimized by terrorism.[53]

Until fairly recently most of the references to assassination and terrorism assumed the connection was that terrorists performed assassinations. Today we find ourselves talking about legitimate heads of state who authorize the targeted killing of specific individuals judged to be terrorist threats. While critics of targeted killing tend to link the practice to assassination because of the legal prohibition of the latter, supporters of targeted killing question whether the accepted wisdom on the topic of assassination is *ad rem*. First of all, active terrorists being targeted are not heads of state, and second, the line between political and military leadership within terrorist groups is often blurry. In times of armed conflict, killing an enemy military leader is not assassination but an acceptable act within a war ethic.

If assassination is understood to mean premeditated killing by an agent of a foreign nation of a political leader *in peacetime*, then the use of the term *assassination* to describe the form of targeted killing enshrined in U.S. counterterrorism policy only confuses the discussion. For the United States understands itself to be involved in an armed conflict with global terrorist organizations, and its legal ban against assassination pertains to peacetime only.

The language of assassination, because it is associated with acts that are widely condemned in the international community and legally banned by the U.S. government, does not help to clarify the ethics of targeted killing in counterterrorism policy. It leads to people on opposite sides of the debate talking past each other, either because there is disagreement about the applicability of the prohibition against assassination (peacetime or armed conflict) or there is no agreement as to whether assassination is always wrong in principle or generally wrong but exceptionally permissible.

During the period 1944–1948 there was an organization, Lehi, that operated across territorial boundaries in the Middle East. It was an organization of Zionists willing to employ assassination and other acts of violence to further their political agenda of establishing an independent Jewish state. One scholar who has studied the organization noted its significance for understanding assassination. This is because the members of Lehi were responsible for two notable assassinations, but also because "they spent considerable time before and after the act analyzing their motives, their deeds, and their impact."[54] Decades later the state of Israel announced a formal policy of targeted killing in its struggle with terrorists. The announcement set off a vigorous debate among Israelis concerned that the new policy was one of state-sponsored assassination. While some opposed the policy, others defended it as a necessary response of self-defense in the face of an organized campaign of terrorism against the Israeli state and society. The next chapter will examine the debate among Israelis as a proximate context for understanding and assessing the U.S. policy of targeted killing.

3

THE PROXIMATE CONTEXT

Israel and the Intifada

An important setting for understanding today's debates on targeted killing is the earlier Israeli policy of what has been variously called "extrajudicial punishment," "selective targeting," or "long-range hot pursuit."[1] The policy, which has become a pillar of Israel's counterterrorism strategy, has been widely debated. A review of the support and opposition to the policy serves as a rehearsal for much of the current debate over the U.S. policy of targeted killing with the use of drones.

The outcome of the Six-Day War in 1967 between Arab nations and Israel was a stunning defeat for the Arab forces. After the war Israel occupied the Sinai Peninsula formerly part of Egypt, the Golan Heights once part of Syria, and the West Bank territories that had been controlled by Jordan. Despite this dramatic turn of events, Palestinian resentment toward Israel was muted by the memory of Jordanian rule in the West Bank and Egyptian governance in Gaza. These past regimes were seen as unhappy arrangements for the Palestinian people. Hence, the Israeli occupation did not cause widespread violence and Palestinian terror activity was only occasional, although sometimes spectacular.[2] The first Palestinian Intifada or uprising (1987–1993), which involved widespread acts of civil disobedience against Israeli authority, did include mass demonstrations but with weapons such as stones and Molotov cocktails. It was a spontaneous civil uprising that had not been planned in advance and sprang from the grassroots more than from the Palestine Liberation Organization (PLO). It was an expression of growing frustration with Israeli occupation and governance of territory that Palestinians hoped would be their sovereign homeland. While specific practical outcomes were not notable, it did lead to greater visibility for the plight of the Palestinian people and their desire for their own homeland.

The second Intifada, begun in September 2000, presented another scenario. It was not really a spontaneous response to the failed Camp David meeting or Israeli prime minister Ariel Sharon's Temple Mount visit, despite attempts to portray it that way. Rather it was a growing and deepening frustration with the lack of movement in resolving the tensions remaining after the Oslo accords of 1993 that set the stage for the second Intifada. The actions or inactions of Sharon, PLO chairman Yassir Arafat, and others in the summer of 2000 were important but they were more like a match set to dry kindling that had already been gathered.[3] In the second Intifada, thousands were killed, both Israeli and Palestinian, and the weapons became far more deadly and sophisticated.

Perhaps no aspect of the second Intifada sowed more terror than the rise of Palestinian suicide bombers used against Israeli civilians in non-battlefield locales. The practice of suicide bombing needs to be understood in order to comprehend the Israeli counterstrategy. The spate of suicide bombers during the second Intifada required a well-orchestrated, disciplined, and financially backed organization. Actual attacks entailed recruitment of bombers, production of the bombs, determining targets, and transportation of the bomber and bomb from the West Bank or Gaza into Israel. The latter element of the strategy was no easy task given Israeli security measures.

Israel had employed targeted killing prior to the second Intifada. In 1956 Israel killed Egyptian intelligence agents who ran operations by fedayeen, Palestinian militants, in Gaza, the West Bank, and Jordan. During the decade of the 1970s there were numerous Israeli targeted killings in reprisal for terrorist attacks. Perhaps the most memorable involved the hunt for those involved in the Munich Olympics murders along with several high-ranking members of the Popular Front for the Liberation of Palestine (PFLP), Hezbollah, Fatah, and al-Saiqa.[4] In some instances, "extrajudicial punishment" may well be the more accurate description of the Israeli action rather than deterrence or preemption of terrorism.[5] With the 1993 Oslo agreement Israel's policy approach to the PLO underwent change, treating it as a potential peace partner rather than implacable enemy. Israel continued to target other organizations such as Hamas and Hezbollah that refused to acknowledge the peace process or Israel's right to exist, but the PLO leadership was no longer subject to military action.

The outbreak of the second Intifada led to a new situation. According to Oslo the Palestinian Authority (PA) and Israel were to be partners in combating terrorism. An important practical consequence was that the PA was expected to arrest and detain terrorist suspects. However, not only did the PA fail to arrest individuals when evidence of terrorist activity was presented by Israelis, but when the Israel Defense Forces (IDF) gave the PA information about a planned arrest the suspects were often alerted so they might escape. The lack of security cooperation, while dozens of suicide attacks killed many Israeli civilians,[6] led the IDF to expand its policy of targeted killing.[7] When individuals were killed in helicopter raids or aerial bombardment, the government of Israel acknowledged its role since it could hardly be denied. However, in cases where a person was killed by long-range sniper fire, gunned down in the street, or killed by a planted bomb, the Israeli government often refused to acknowledge any role in the death.

As might be expected, the Israeli policy became the subject of significant debate both within and without Israel. Two killings in particular set off firestorms of charges and countercharges. On December 31, 2000, a West Bank dentist was killed by the IDF. Dr. Thabet Ahmad Thabet did not fit the classic terrorist profile: he was a human rights activist, director general of the Palestinian health ministry, and was widely known and befriended by many in Israel's Peace Now movement. Two weeks prior to his killing he had passed through Ben-Gurion Airport without incident.[8] The IDF claimed that he was, in effect, a Jekyll and Hyde who, despite his peaceful persona, was actually in his Mr. Hyde mode a regional commander of a unit of Palestinian gunmen.

Thabet's widow filed a petition with the Israeli High Court to order the cessation of the policy of targeted killings. In response a team of lawyers for the IDF wrote a brief claiming that the dispute with the Palestinians had escalated to an extent that it was no longer a domestic dispute between an occupying force and the resident population, but an armed conflict governed by the norms that apply to war between states.

One of the IDF advisors, Daniel Reisner, argued that targeted killings were permissible under six conditions: (1) the intended target is a combatant in the armed conflict; (2) arrest of the target is not possible; (3) senior civilian officials approve the targeted killing; (4) care for civilian casualties is governed by the norm of proportionality; (5) the targeted killing occurs in an area not under Israeli control; and (6) the target is deemed a future threat, not just a perpetrator of past crime.[9] Reisner sought to put the targeted killing policy into a context of legal regulation and political accountability.

The IDF in explaining and defending its policy made it clear that it had adopted criteria drawn from the just war tradition to govern its implementation of the policy of targeted killing. First, the PA must ignore requests that the individual be arrested. Second, the IDF must determine that it is unable to make an arrest itself. Both of these elements are related to the idea of last resort in just war. Third, the killing must be done to prevent an imminent attack or future attack, not for revenge or retribution. This stricture is related to just cause and right intent.

A development in the Thabet case was that the Israeli government was public in acknowledging its targeted killing. It also announced a limit to targeted killings, stating that the policy was aimed at terrorists, not political leaders. Nonetheless, less than a year after the death of Thabet, in August 2001, there was a deadly attack upon Abu Ali Mustafa, the leader of the political side of the PFLP. The targeted killing operation was approved by the government of Prime Minister Ariel Sharon because Shin Bet, the Israeli intelligence agency, convinced top Israeli rulers that Mustafa was actively involved in terror attacks. A member of the Israeli defense sector stated that Israel did not target Mustafa as a political leader but because of his personal involvement with attacks.

Then the following summer, in July 2002, the IDF dropped a one-ton bomb that killed Salah Shahada, the leader of Hamas's military wing, allegedly responsible for the deaths of more than 220 Israeli civilians in more than fifty attacks. However, in the Israeli attack 15 civilians died along with Shahada, including 9 children. The attacks underscored several criticisms raised about the Israeli policy: (1) how were targets identified and with what certitude? (2) were the attacks being carried out with sufficient concern for the traditional norms of discrimination and proportionality?

ISRAELI PUBLIC DEBATE

One of the earliest commentators on the Israeli policy was Gal Luft, an Israeli political scientist, who has lived for years in the United States working as an advisor and consultant on issues in the Middle East. Writing in 2003 he stated that in the first two years of the second Intifada there had been "at least eighty" instances of targeted killing against Palestinian militants.[10] Acknowledging there are shortcomings to the policy, and that critics view the practice as illegal and senseless, Luft argues that the targeted killing policy has been effective. The benefit of the policy is best understood in its cumulative effect upon terrorist organizations.

For Luft there are two important points to remember about the targeted killing policy. First, although the threat of terror is ongoing, that should not lead to doubts about the efficacy of the policy. The impact of the policy upon terrorist organizations must be assessed over time, for the regular elimination of terrorist leaders has a cumulative impact: it interrupts planning, communication, recruitment, and training that gradually takes a toll upon the terrorist organization. Defenders of targeted killing make this point about the cumulative toll of a targeted killing policy often. Second, it is difficult for the Israeli government to discuss the lives saved by the thwarting of terrorist plans. One Israeli calculation is that each terrorist death amounts to saving sixteen to twenty Israeli lives.[11]

That people in Israel were able to return to normal daily activities is due, at least in part, to the demise of those who otherwise would have been killing Israeli civilians.[12]

Luft was not blind to the downsides of the policy. When the wrong target is identified there are serious repercussions for Israel's reputation and for its diplomatic efforts. The targeted killing policy has allowed factions within the Palestinian community to use the policy as a cover for killings that are due to domestic rivalries. As well, the policy has encouraged Palestinian resolve to retaliate in a deadly tit for tat and established Israeli political and military leaders as likely targets for terrorist strikes. Luft's essay touched upon a number of themes that would be discussed and debated by subsequent writers on the topic of targeted killing.

Stephen David and Yael Stein

Another early and influential essay defending Israel's policy was that of Steven David of Johns Hopkins University. An exchange between David and Yael Stein, research director of B'Tselem, the Israeli Information Center for Human Rights in the Occupied Territories, illustrated the disagreement and the range of issues entailed. David argued that targeted killing, "the intentional slaying of a specific individual or group of individuals undertaken with explicit governmental approval," is not the same as assassination, an act that he agrees should be banned.[13] The key distinctions for David are that assassination commonly uses treacherous means and takes place in times of peace. Regarding the first distinction, David argued that while there have been uses of deception by the IDF in its killings, the overwhelming number of IDF actions have been openly military.

Concerning the description of the setting as peace or war, David argues that international law is insufficiently nuanced for the present age. Legally, Israel is not at war since war is characterized by a struggle between two armies or two states. The Palestinians have neither, but Israel clearly is engaged in armed conflict and, if that is so, then it may target combatants. International law has not caught up with the rise of global terrorism. For David, this is key because it is not assassination to target those who may be counted as combatants. International law does not prohibit the killing of those who direct or lead armed forces in combat. Targeted killing, therefore, is simply another legitimate form of killing during war or armed conflict.

Is it true that Palestinians engaged in terror activities are proper targets? For David, the question does not turn on the existence of a regular, uniformed army representing a state. Clearly, if that was a necessary condition it would render the Palestinians noncombatants. However, for David, "[w]hat is critical is whether the objects of the targeted killings pose an armed threat to Israeli security."[14] Since those targeted are members of militant groups that call for the destruction of Israel and undertake armed attacks against the Israeli people, they should be considered combatants. Even civilians, after all, can be considered combatants if they are part of the military chain of command, according to most international jurists.

In sum, for David, the Israeli policy is not the equivalent of assassination. Israel "is engaged in armed conflict with terrorists, those targeted are often killed by conventional military means, and the targets are mostly combatants or are part of the military chain of command."[15] In cases that do not fit those criteria the killings may be equivalent to assassination, but the majority of targeted killings since the second Intifada do fit the criteria and, therefore, the Israeli policy is not a policy of assassination in violation of international law or common morality.

Yael Stein responded to David's defense of targeted killing by arguing that the Israeli policy is an ethical and legal violation of accepted norms. Stein disputes the claim that the Palestinians targeted "meet the legal definition of combatants." She also believes that the policy relies far more heavily upon treachery than David admits. The majority of the cases "required the cooperation of Palestinian collaborators and informers" and such cooperation was "usually obtained through the use of illegal means such as threats to the collaborators or their families, extortion, or bribes."[16]

Stein challenges her government's classification of the Palestinian targets as "illegal combatants," arguing that international law knows only combatants and civilians. Stein argues that Israel does not treat the Palestinians as combatants since it does not accord them prisoner of war status, nor does it see the killing of Israeli soldiers by the Palestinians as legitimate acts of war. She notes that "civilians who participate in hostilities lose their immunity and become legitimate targets" according to the Geneva Convention. "Yet, this is only true for the time they take active part in the hostilities" and once they halt such activity they regain their civilian status, that is, they no longer have a right to kill and they are no longer legitimate targets.[17]

Civilians who have taken up weapons and participated in past hostilities may be arrested and prosecuted under the penal law of the arresting country, but they are to be treated as indicted criminals in custody. "They cannot be hunted down and summarily executed."[18] Since Israel has never presented evidence that its targets have been actively participating in hostilities in the legal sense of present combat activity, the killings done under its targeted killing policy are illegal.

Morally, the policy fails to satisfy basic norms for the taking of life, according to Stein. She points out that about one-third of those killed in targeted killings have been innocent bystanders. Further, she maintains that the implementation of the policy is deeply flawed not only for the risk to third parties, but also for the risk of mistakes in choosing targets. The selection "could be based on unreliable or mistaken information about the actual or potential actions performed by this person and about the danger he poses."[19] If the criminal justice system can make mistakes, how much more the risk for a secretive, nonadversarial process where the accused has no opportunity to rebut charges.

When she turns to the moral as distinct from the legal arguments, Stein challenges David's approval of the targeted killing policy on several fronts. First, she questions the discriminate and proportionate nature of the policy since one-third of those "killed in the course of these attacks so far have been innocent bystanders, according to the army's own admission."[20] Second, Stein challenges the claims that just cause and right intent govern the Israeli policy. David himself acknowledges that the policy "affords the Israeli public a calibrated form of revenge," and that targeted killing "is a form of controlled, state-sanctioned revenge."[21] He also employs a retribution argument as justified "because it is through this approach that the terrorists get what they inflict on others."[22]

Stein rejects both of these arguments as satisfying just cause and right intent according to the just war tradition. In her view such "feelings" cannot guide state behavior for states must be bound by law. David's arguments may accurately describe the real reason behind the targeted killing policy but it is not a rationale that Israel wants to admit. "When Israel emphasizes that these killings are preventive rather than punitive measures, it does so for a reason: punishment without trial is illegal and immoral."[23] Without reference to Luft, Stein makes a point that challenges his outlook as well as David's. "The effectiveness of the policy is irrelevant to either its legality or its morality." Denying people their basic human rights cannot be explained away because it attains a result that a public official desires.[24]

In a rebuttal David suggests that the divide between himself and Stein is a matter of vision. For Stein the clarity of either-or legal categories determines the way to describe the situation. For David, the legal issues are far more ambiguous because "international law applies best to situations of war and peace between recognized states. Targeted killing, however, takes place in a context that is neither war nor peace, between belligerents, one of which is not a state."[25]

David challenges Stein's rejection of targeted killing as meeting the standard of proportionality due to the deaths of innocents. For David, targeted killing, "when carried out correctly, minimizes such casualties" and is "a preferable option to bombing or large-scale military sweeps" into the occupied territories, for those strategies generate great harm to noncombatants. Admittedly, the situation would be greatly altered if the PA were "willing to cooperate in bringing terrorists to justice" for then there would be a reasonable alternative, thereby delegitimating targeted killing.[26] Sadly, for David, that reasonable alternative has not come to pass.

In closing the exchange, David agrees with Stein's worries about the procedures involved in targeted killing and accepts that Israel "should do more to prevent errors, think more carefully about deciding whom to target, and work harder to create a process with greater transparency and civilian oversight." He concludes that "where we disagree is that I believe the policy can be fixed, whereas Stein simply wants it abolished."[27]

From this early exchange between commentators on the Israeli policy it is possible to identify several topics that will require resolution in the ethical debate regarding targeted killing.

- Does international law adequately categorize the nature of combatant and noncombatant identity in the case of international terrorism?
- Do criteria drawn from the just war tradition provide sufficient guidance for informing moral judgments about targeted killing in counterterrorist campaigns?
- What is the status of those Palestinians involved in a variety of roles that enable terrorist attacks upon Israeli citizens? (This latter question is a more specific formulation of the first question.)
- What is the weight to be given to claims of efficacy in an ethical analysis of targeted killing policy? Should it be decisive? Significant? Beside the point?
- Is targeted killing a form of assassination banned by international law?
- Are the procedures employed in Israel's targeted killing policy adequate to ensure against mistakes in target selection and actual operation of a targeted killing?

Michael Gross and Daniel Statman

A second substantive exchange occasioned by the Israeli policy took place through a series of essays by Michael Gross, a political scientist at the University of Haifa, and his colleague in the university's philosophy department, Daniel Statman.

In an essay published in 2003, Gross expressed great reservation about Israel's policy. His first point was that the use of lethal force is permissible in two realms, law enforcement and just war. At the outset of the targeted killing policy Israel attempted to justify its actions as a permissible form of law enforcement. The ordinary processes of law enforcement involve infiltration, intelligence, arrest, and detention. And so the inappropriateness of this law enforcement model was soon clear when questions about the targeted killing policy were posed concerning the lack of due process, a clear premeditated intent to kill, the reality of retribution as motive, and the absence of review procedures. Such concerns demonstrated the feeble analogy of the targeted killing policy with the law enforcement paradigm.[28]

Israel then redefined its relationship with the Palestinians as one of armed conflict rather than "belligerent occupation." By so doing Palestinian militia were transformed into combatants and not criminals, thereby acting within the protections of the Geneva Conventions. Gross suggests that Israel traded an unconvincing policy of "extralegal" execution for a dubious policy of assassination that is a violation of the laws of war and an incitement to further terrorist acts.[29]

Dropping the pretext of law enforcement did allow the Israelis to claim that the targeted killings were legitimate military attacks upon permissible targets. Gross challenges that claim, however. He notes that targeted killing as a strategy of armed conflict must satisfy criteria analogous to those of just war theory. First, there must be a just reason and Gross suggests this entails self-defense. Targeted killing, therefore, ought to be focused on the interdiction of terrorists and not directed toward retribution or punishment. Second, there must be a reasonable conviction that success in stopping the particular individual would halt the terrorist act. "This demands knowledge that the suspect is not only preparing an attack but is so instrumentally involved that only his death can prevent it."[30] Finally, proportionality suggests that the cost of a targeted killing policy must consider the cost it exacts due to the fierce spirit of resistance and retaliation it inspires.

Daniel Statman, colleague and friend of Gross, thinks that the presumed evil of assassination needs to be reconsidered. For Statman, assassination is actually preferable to other forms of killing in war where people are killed anonymously or en masse as "collateral damage," or simply because they are "the enemy." Targeted killing, on the other hand, attacks specific individuals "because they bear personal responsibility or play a special role" in aggression.[31]

Statman also makes the point that proportionality ought not be assessed simply on the basis of the lack of short-term benefits compared to costs. "[I]n the war against terror, just like the war against the mafia, what counts are long-term results, not the immediate ones." Statman acknowledges that the short-term consequence of the targeted killing policy might be an increase in retaliatory attacks. But it is possible the policy "will weaken the terror organizations, cause demoralization among their members, limit their movements," and diminish terrorism over time.[32]

In this way of viewing the matter Statman agrees with Luft and David that killing recruiters, bomb makers, passport forgers, travel facilitators, and others beyond the actual suicide bombers removes people whose skills cannot easily be replaced. It is possible to drain the pool of skilled terrorists. With an effective targeted killing campaign, terrorists spend much time in hiding or moving from place to place. Communication by phone becomes risky, the circle of trusted colleagues shrinks, meetings or training sessions are harder to arrange and pull off. Energy is spent investigating possible "moles" and informers. In sum, there are fewer leaders to lead and less time and opportunity for plotting and preparation of attacks, while organizational cohesion and motivation also wane. Targeted killing is but a part of a counterterrorism strategy, but its effectiveness as a long-term strategy may be underestimated when the timeframe for assessment is solely immediate.

In a later and longer response to Gross's objection to Israel's policy of targeted killing, Statman argued that accepting "the legitimacy of the killing and destruction in a conventional war necessarily entails accepting the legitimacy of targeted killing in the war against terror."[33] At the outset of his argument Statman proposes that the proper context for assessing the Israeli policy is not law enforcement but that of war. This is so for two reasons: (1) the second Intifada is an organized and systematic series of near daily attacks upon civilians that has established a clear basis for Israel declaring the necessity of exercising its right of self-defense; and (2) the law enforcement model is manifestly impractical given the PA's refusal to assist in stopping the terrorist activity, thereby rendering the armed conflict a matter of last resort.[34]

If the struggle against armed organizations such as Hamas, Tanzim, and similar groups can be described as war, then it follows that Israel may use lethal means to kill members of these aggressive forces. Admittedly, these fighters are irregular combatants, not typical combatants according to the conventions of war, yet their active participation in armed organizations renders them far more like combatants than civilians. Just as members of the armed forces of conventional armies at war may target and kill one another, so may the IDF target and kill members of terrorist organizations.

Indeed, members of terrorist organizations are even more legitimately targeted since many conventional forces are composed of conscripts forced to fight, whereas the terrorist groups rely upon volunteer members who subscribe to the aims and methods of the organization. Targeted killing demonstrates a more discriminate and proportionate response to terror attacks than invasions of the occupied territories or neighboring states that serve as shelters for the terror groups. And there is less risk to civilians than would be the case with extensive artillery or bombing campaigns.

Statman's argument goes beyond the calculation of saving the lives of civilians, as important as that is, for he makes the point that targeted killing "is more commensurate with a fundamental condition of justified self-defense, namely that those killed are responsible for the threat posed."[35] The Israeli policy "expresses the appropriate respect for human life during wartime" since with targeted killing "human beings are killed not simply because they are 'the enemy,' but because they bear special responsibility or play a special role in the enemy's aggression."[36] Targeted killing, in effect, requires a more discriminate form of targeting than the usual methods employed in warfare.

If in a conventional war snipers may be deployed to kill enemy combatants hiding in a residential building, so in counterterrorism targeted killing may be employed against terrorists who set up hideouts and residences amid civilians. For Statman, the policy of targeted killing is an example of taking *jus in bello* norms seriously since the attacks limit noncombatant deaths and are far more discriminate and proportionate than other conventional strategies. According to Statman, if you can kill in a conventional war you can engage in targeted killing against terrorists.[37]

An additional and important issue that Statman takes up is the fact that targeted killings often take place in settings that are not designated as combat zones. If a military chief of staff can be attacked in his office by means of long-range artillery or aerial bombardment this is generally viewed as acceptable according to the norms of conventional war. But, Statman asks, what if the military leader is not in his office but on a family vacation? Is it morally acceptable that a sniper might shoot to kill? If A may kill B in self-defense when B poses a serious threat to A, and B cannot be restrained in any other way than being killed, it does not appear as if B's location should make a difference. It would be a relevant factor if self-defense is only permissible against a direct and imminent threat. But in conventional war there is a wider license to kill the enemy: "[S]oldiers and officers can be killed while asleep, while doing office work, or while out on maneuvers."[38]

Indeed, the majority of soldiers involved in office work, transportation behind the lines, or resting while off-duty cannot plausibly be described as posing an imminent and direct threat. And yet by the standards of conventional warfare there is no war crime involved if a sniper, artillery officer, or fighter pilot attacks an enemy military base. There have been instances where ground rules such as not targeting generals or not attacking soldiers away from the combat zone are involved, but these, Statman argues, are conventions that combatants agree upon to limit the suffering and death of warfare. However, the moral force of a convention "is contingent on its being followed by all sides," according to Statman. "[R]ules based on convention differ from rules founded on strict moral grounds, which are obligatory regardless of what the other side does."[39] To avoid deliberately targeting innocent children is an example of a moral norm that must be obeyed regardless of what the enemy does, but not killing combatants away from the battle lines is a convention that can be waived if the other side does not respect it.

In a later and wide-ranging essay, Michael Gross returns to the issue of what paradigm should be employed when assessing targeted killing. Is it best seen as an act of self-defense or better understood from the vantage of law enforcement? In both paradigms it is considered legitimate to use deadly force, but the law enforcement paradigm places significant restrictions upon a police officer's use of force since the target is presumed innocent and due process is required to establish guilt. Only highly threatening circumstances permit killing in self-defense within the law enforcement model. The norms of war allow soldiers to use deadly force against enemy soldiers with far less restraints than those placed on the police officer. So the ethical assessment of targeted killing largely depends, says Gross, upon the status one gives to terrorists.

Gross makes the point that developments in modern war, particularly the prevalence of asymmetric warfare, have blurred the applicability of the laws of war. In fact, in 1977 Protocols I and II of the Geneva Conventions were revised to address the question of combatant status in contemporary warfare.[40] As the distinction between combatants and civilians blurs, will soldiers decide if nonuniformed persons are really civilians and so avoid harming them, or will soldiers assume that many civilians are really nonuniformed combatants and thereby subject to being harmed? As Michael Walzer once observed, soldiers must feel secure amid civilians if civilians are to feel safe among soldiers. Any loosening of the Geneva protocols regarding who may be counted as a legitimate combatant means the risks to both combatants and civilians increase.

Gross believes it defies common sense to suggest that a person is no longer a combatant simply because he or she has left the battlefield or is not carrying a weapon. The terrorist cannot be granted a status change by simple gestures that can be quickly and easily reversed once there is no risk involved. Furthermore, terrorists may continue to be at work as "they prepare for battle, lay plans, tend to their weapons and maintain their fighting capability."[41] After all, the terrorist threat is not reducible solely to the actual operational behavior of a suicide bomber; rather, the terrorism includes all the moments and actors within the complex and sometimes extended process involved in launching an attack.

The challenge is to determine an individual's status absent the traditional markings of uniforms, insignia, and weapons. Here Gross suggests that the process of compiling a list of known terrorists such as takes place with a policy of targeted killing can be understood as an attempt to establish whether a person should be designated a combatant or civilian. If identified as a combatant then he or she is vulnerable in the same way that a uniformed combatant is a legitimate target of attack.[42]

For Gross, the war paradigm, though not without its problems, ends up being the more apt context for discussing terrorists. The simple reality is that "terrorists pose grave material threats to civilian populations. . . . For the purpose of assessing a threat and targeting it accordingly, it is not necessary to consider that terrorists are acting unlawfully or immorally." What Israel did was similar to what any nation does; it "sizes up the threat it faces and then considers how best to defend itself."[43] Hence, targeted killing may be considered an act of legitimate self-defense. But there remain other criteria from the just war tradition that still must be weighed: necessity (last resort), utility (reasonable hope of success), and proportionality.[44]

These criteria lead Gross to ponder whether targeted killings are necessary to protect Israel from the threat of terror assaults. Might other methods, even nonmilitary strategies, be successful in diminishing the threat of terror? What is to count as success in this context—security for Israeli citizens, disabling terror organizations, progress toward peace? Does a policy of targeted killing enhance all of these to the same degree? In a six-year period from 2000 to 2006, the IDF carried out 204 targeted killings, killing 113 civilians in the process of implementing the policy. Is that reasonable "collateral damage" or does such a ratio inflame and radicalize more Palestinians? Gross continues to harbor doubts that the Israeli policy can satisfy such concerns, at least in many cases.

Daniel Statman also returned to the topic of targeted killing in a later essay.[45] He begins by noting that most of the writing on targeted killing has assumed a legal point of view, assuming that if it is legally justified it is morally right as well. Instead he explicitly wishes to examine targeted killing from the perspective of the moral tradition of just war thinking and examines three different interpretations of that tradition as posed by contemporary philosophers. He concludes that each of the three variant readings of the tradition supports the practice of targeted killing.[46]

The three main interpretations among philosophers of the just war tradition are identified as individualism, collectivism, and contractualism. Statman seeks to answer the same question from each of these understandings of the tradition: "is targeted killing a legitimate means of warfare given that the war of which it is a part is just?"[47]

Individualism proposes that permission to kill in war is similar to the license to kill in individual self-defense. That is, one must show the targeted individual posed an unjust threat, was morally responsible for doing so, that there was no other way to stop the threat, and that the death caused was not disproportionate to the evil avoided. In this first interpretation the key is responsibility; is the individual responsible for presenting an unjust threat?

Collectivism posits that war cannot be understood as simply a set of individual confrontations; they are necessarily conflicts between collectives that are initiated and fought by individuals who represent the collectives. When a soldier is killed it is not as an individual but as an agent of the opposing collective. For the collectivist the key issue is participation: is the targeted combatant a participant in the collective's war effort?

Contractualism suggests that any state has an interest in reducing the evil of war while also maintaining the ability to effectively defend itself against an aggressor. So states have agreed that combatants may be killed with few restrictions while noncombatants may not be directly killed, with few exceptions. War entails people giving up their natural right not to be killed; it is not about individual desert or liability, but the key is the mutual forfeiture of rights.[48]

Statman then distinguishes three groups: innocents, such as young children, who are no threat at all; adult noncombatants, some of whom may contribute to the unjust threat; and combatants. All three models agree the presumption against attacking the innocent stands, and all three models accept the distinction between combatants and noncombatants as valid, though for different reasons. Finally, individualism attaches no great moral significance to whether the context for killing is war since the same rules apply in or out of war; whereas collectivism attaches crucial significance to the context since in war a whole group of people (combatants) lose their immunity from attack. Contractualism, too, sees the determination of whether the context is war or not as central, since the moral convention that is the *jus in bello* only pertains to the context of war.[49]

For the individualist, the central concern is whether the person is responsible for an unjust threat. It does not matter if the terrorist is described as a soldier or criminal, a member of a terrorist organization or not. What is crucial is that the person poses a serious threat to the life of another individual. If so, then targeted killing might not only be permissible but preferred in the individualist reading, for it lessens the "collateral damage" of nontargeted killing, that is, conventional methods such as invasion or aerial bombardment.[50]

Within the collectivist framework of just war thinking, the vital concern is whether there are two collectives engaged in armed conflict. Certainly the IDF represents a collective. Does an organization like Hamas also merit such a designation? Statman argues that Hamas can reasonably be described as a militant organization representing the collective body of the Palestinian people in Gaza. Furthermore, given that membership in Hamas is voluntary and not by conscription, it is also evident that individuals who join Hamas with its public threat of terrorism toward Israel can be understood as assuming responsibility for a deadly threat to Israeli civilians. So both the individualist and the collectivist can support targeted killings as self-defense against members of Hamas.[51]

The third interpretive model of the just war tradition, contractualism, ordinarily presumes that the war convention is an agreement between states. Yet there is no reason why it must be limited in that manner. The rules of *jus in bello* are mutually beneficial not just for states but for liberation movements or any group that takes up arms to fight against perceived oppression. Is targeted killing an action that is governed by a mutually agreed upon convention for fighting? Statman claims that "targeted killing is aimed at people who are actively involved in planning and carrying out perceived unjust threats to other people, hence they are liable to defensive attack against them."[52] Thus, there is nothing inherently wrong with targeted killing, and if it is wrong it is so only by convention. If a nation decides not to abide by a conventional norm, that is a legitimate decision as long as it continues to abide by basic norms of morality that are not merely conventional, for example, no direct attacks upon children.

Reviewing the exchange between Gross and Statman it is possible to see further refinement in the Israeli public discussion as well as the continuation of unanswered questions that allow for ongoing debate.

- There is movement away from viewing the law enforcement paradigm as the most appropriate way to discuss Israel's counterterrorism policy. A number of voices, even among those initially skeptical, see the context as being that of armed conflict. The terror attacks were not sporadic and isolated but organized, systematic, and occurred with regularity.
- Also, the inability or unwillingness of the Palestinian Authority to cooperate in the identification and arrest of those committing terrorist acts made law enforcement procedures difficult to implement.
- Are terrorists to be considered ordinary combatants with the privileges as well as risks that such status entails? For example, granting prisoner of war status to those apprehended and the right of those captured not to cooperate in interrogation? If terrorists are neither regular combatants nor innocent civilians, when do they become noncombatants? Is a careful process of determining a "kill list" of

specific named targets the means whereby combatant status is to be determined?

- In the armed conflict paradigm the criteria for moral assessment of Israel's policy may be drawn from the just war tradition. That requires a determination of self-defense as a just cause, but also entails concern for other norms such as last resort or necessity, utility or reasonable hope of success, and proportionality or minimal collateral damage.
- Determining what counts as success or utility is an open question. There is a growing appreciation that targeted killing is to be judged by its cumulative effect in undermining or destroying the ability of terrorists to launch successful attacks upon Israeli civilians.
- Long-term, is the targeted killing policy to be deemed a success because of the lessening of terrorist attacks? Or must it be seen as necessary for the defeat of groups such as Hamas and others that do not recognize Israel? Or even more broadly, is targeted killing, as part of a counterterrorism strategy, to be assessed by whether it is helpful or harmful to the furtherance of the Mideast peace process?
- Does the decision to approve a targeted killing require assignment of individual responsibility for wrongdoing? Does membership in certain organizations that sponsor terrorism provide sufficient reason to approve a targeted killing?
- Are there declared battlefields or combat zones where targeted killing is permitted, and outside of which targeted killing is forbidden? Is the expectation of bounded areas for armed conflict a fundamental tenet of moral combat or a war convention that binds only if there is reciprocity in observance?

Other Israeli Voices

Amos Guiora, a former member of the Judge Advocate General Corps of the IDF, advocated what he called "active self-defense," by which he meant an approach similar to what others call anticipatory self-defense or preemptive self-defense. Given the nature of terrorist attacks, Israel, or any state seeking an effective defense, "must be able to take the fight to the terrorist before the terrorist takes the fight to it."[53] This is, admittedly, a somewhat different approach than the UN Charter approves in Article 51, where self-defense is invoked only if an attack occurs. Guiora maintains that earlier customary international law allowed for anticipatory self-defense or active self-defense "as long as the threat to national security is reasonably believed to be imminent."[54] It is his argument that the present narrower interpretation of self-defense in international law is less applicable to the new asymmetric sort of armed conflict that global terror networks create. Further, Guiora maintains that targeted killing is one of the major elements in a policy of active self-defense.

An acceptable policy of targeted killing must be circumscribed by moral boundaries. Targeted killing must be used solely to prevent terrorist attacks; it is not to be employed as a means of reprisal or punishment for past acts. Also, it is to be used only when arrest or capture is not an option. For Guiora this distinguishes targeted killing from extrajudicial killing.[55] In addition, the practice of any targeted killing must be in accord with the existing legal and moral norms regarding proportionality, military necessity, collateral damage, and lack of less harmful options.

Based on his personal experience in overseeing the IDF in its counterterrorism operations, Guiora argues that targeted killing (1) can lessen the collateral damage that accompanies more conventional military operations; (2) is necessary for the defense of Israeli civilians; (3) has in most cases been proportionate in the balance of good that is done over harm caused; and (4) is not pursued if there are other less lethal measures available to stop a terrorist attack.

The other key piece in Guiora's proposal is the question of who may be targeted. Like earlier participants in the public debate, he believes terrorists who take a direct role in attacks upon Israeli civilians are combatants in an armed conflict and subject to being targeted. Such terrorists are, however, "illegal combatants" not entitled to POW status. "Furthermore, the legitimate target is not limited to the potential suicide bomber who, according to corroborated and reliable intelligence is 'on his way' to carrying out a suicide bombing. Rather the legitimate target is identified as a Palestinian that plays a significant role in the suicide bomber infrastructure."[56]

Guiora closes his essay with an appeal for the need to revise international law to better account for armed conflict between states and organized terror networks. Just as the Geneva Conventions were shaped as a result of the experience of World War II, there is a need that an updated international law "explicitly providing for active self-defense should be formed out of what has been learned from Israel's struggle with terrorism."[57]

Asa Kasher, the former commander of the IDF College of National Defense, and Amos Yadlin, a university professor of philosophy who also advises the IDF College, contributed an essay that defends a policy similar to Guiora's active self-defense, although they refer to it as preventive killing. The authors take care to distinguish why such a policy is not one of assassination. Kasher and Yadlin define assassination as "an act of killing a prominent person selectively, intentionally, and for political (including religious) purposes."[58] They then proceed to explain what they see as Israel's rationale for the practice of targeted killing.

The first principle to be invoked is the duty of self-defense, the prime duty of a democratic state with regard to its citizens.[59] The second principle is that of military necessity, when the state must use armed force to defend the lives of its citizens in accord with five conditions. First is that the purpose is to fulfill the basic duty of defending citizens' lives. Second, that any alternative to using armed force would expose citizens to greater danger. Third, that any use of force is done in a manner that minimizes all collateral damage to persons not directly involved in terrorism. Fourth, that there be an accounting of the relationship between the effective defense of citizens and the collateral damage caused. Finally, that the decision to use force is not special pleading but would be justifiable in all incidents of similar situations.[60]

The third and final principle Kasher and Yadlin invoke is that of distinction, whereby they enumerate the different duties incumbent upon the state with regard to those persons who are neither citizens nor residents of the state and who may have no involvement in terror, or are indirectly involved in terror, or who are directly involved in terrorism. The authors proceed to distinguish what counts as instances of direct versus indirect terror involvement.[61]

Essentially, the authors argue that targeted killing can be justified, even if there is some collateral damage caused, if the target was directly engaged in operations for a forthcoming terrorist attack, there were no reasonable alternatives to the use of targeted killing to stop the attack, and the collateral damage was not disproportionate to the benefit attained by the attack.

A controversial aspect of the proposal by Kasher and Yadlin is their willingness to argue that Israel must give the lives of Israeli citizens, including the military, a priority over the lives of non-Israeli combatants and civilians when assessing proportionality and collateral damage. This would seem to contradict the widely held view within the just war tradition that soldiers must be willing to put themselves at risk rather than innocent civilians.[62] Kasher and Yadlin also confusingly close their essay by defending the case of assassination of a prominent person if that individual is implicated in direct involvement in terrorist activity. However, it would appear that the basis for an act of targeted killing in such a case would be as an act of self-defense on the part of the state rather than an act of killing for political purposes. Therefore it would not be an assassination as they had previously defined the term.

Two final contributions to the public debate over the policy of targeted killing that took place in Israel come from an international lawyer at Hebrew University in Jerusalem and a political scientist at Tel Aviv University. The lawyer, David Kretzmer, examines whether a targeted killing of a terrorist is best viewed as a legitimate means of self-defense or as an extrajudicial execution. As with other authors we have examined, Kretzmer sees the issue of targeted killings as being "a fundamental disagreement not only regarding their morality or legality, but also on the issue of the legal regime by which that legality should be judged."[63] Those who favor a law enforcement model for assessing the issue tend toward a negative judgment on targeted killing, seeing it as extrajudicial killing, while those who view the situation through the lens of armed conflict tend toward the view that targeted killing ought to be assessed by the criteria of the just war tradition and the international laws governing warfare.

For Kretzmer, the major drawback with the law enforcement model is that "one of its fundamental premises is invalid: that the suspected perpetrator is within the jurisdiction of the law-enforcement authorities"[64] so that an arrest can be made. He acknowledges that a suspected terrorist does not lose his right to life and cannot be arbitrarily targeted for death simply because he lives outside the territory of the victim state. Kretzmer suggests, however, that "when there is strong evidence that the suspected terrorist is actually planning terrorist attacks against the victim state, and there is no feasible way of preventing those attacks by apprehending or arresting him," then a targeted killing "would not necessarily be regarded as an arbitrary deprivation of life."[65] That is, targeted killing would be legitimate in principle, but other criteria, such as norms of just warfare, must be considered in each particular case. By appealing to standards derived from the just war tradition there is an obvious movement beyond the law enforcement paradigm to that of armed conflict.

If one adopts the model of armed conflict for examining counterterrorism and targeted killing, there are still other problems to consider. At present, Kretzmer states that international law governs two possible scenarios. First is that the terrorist attack and the armed response of the victim state "has created an international armed conflict between the victim state and the host state" in which the terrorists abide. Or second, that "an armed conflict has been created between the victim state and the terrorist group," independent of whether there is a conflict between host and victim states. Yet the prevailing interpretation of the law of *international* armed conflict is that it is a conflict between *states*. And the situation contemplated of noninternational armed conflict is that of conflict within a state, between a government and rebels within the territory. In sum, the norms of international humanitarian law that govern armed conflict "do not apply to a conflict between a state and a terrorist group acting from outside its territory."[66]

In addition, the norms of international humanitarian law presume a binary option regarding the status of individuals; one is either a combatant or a civilian. Terrorists do not easily fit into either category since they violate at least three of the four criteria that the Geneva Conventions lay out for combatant status: being under responsible command; wearing a fixed distinctive sign or uniform; carrying weapons openly; and abiding by the laws and customs of war, which, among other things, prohibit the targeting of civilians.[67]

So if not combatants, are terrorists to be considered civilians? That seems to fly in the face of commonsense experience. Are they only liable to armed resistance when they are in the operational act of a terror attack but immediately before or after such an act are to be considered civilians and accorded all the immunities that civilians have under the laws of war? This is what Kretzmer and others call the "revolving door" theory, whereby terrorists are provided the best of both worlds. "They can remain civilians most of the time and only endanger their protection as civilians while actually in the process of carrying out a terrorist act."[68]

For the above reasons, as well as other reservations Kretzmer describes in his careful and comprehensive approach, the author concludes that neither the law enforcement model nor the armed conflict model is adequate for addressing global terror. The first model is "not suitable when the scale of violence has reached that of a non-international armed conflict and the terrorists operate from a state that is either unwilling or incapable of cooperating in law enforcement." The second model of armed conflict was not developed with global terror in mind since under its norms "terrorists are generally not combatants and may therefore only be attacked for such time as they take a direct part in hostilities," a conclusion that overlooks the existence of an organized terrorist group that has declared war on a victim state.[69]

Kretzmer concludes that what is needed to address the situation in Israel is a "mixed model" that "incorporates elements of the laws of belligerent occupation, active armed conflict and international human rights."[70] The reason for this is that the existing paradigms are not adequate for effective guidance for the Israeli state in conducting an ethical, legal, and effective counterterrorism strategy. Treating "suspected transnational terrorists as civilians who at times take part in hostilities is an unrealistic perception of the situation." It will not be effective. Yet treating terrorists as "combatants who may be targeted at will opens the way to serious violations of the right to life in non-international armed conflict." Such a policy will not be ethical or legal. Kretzmer seeks a middle road "that allows states to defend their residents against terror attacks without abandoning commitment to standards of human rights and humanitarian law."[71]

Tamar Meisels, a political scientist, strongly argues for treating terrorists as combatants, but unlawful combatants. Such "irregular belligerents" are "ineligible either for the immunities guaranteed to soldiers by international conventions of war or for the protections of the criminal justice system."[72] Lawful combatants, of course, are entitled to the war rights of soldiers, specifically prisoner of war status if captured, which includes the right to refuse interrogation beyond name, rank, and serial number as well as provision of basic levels of humane care while in custody. Unless personally responsible for war crimes, individual soldiers cannot be put on trial and held criminally culpable for fighting in a war.[73]

Meisels maintains that terrorists should not qualify for any of these protections because they are guilty of "subverting the most fundamental rules of war, whose purpose is to protect the civilian population by specifying for each individual a single identity: either soldier or civilian."[74] Unlawful combatants are wrong in two ways. "First, they threaten the well-being of the surrounding population by blurring the distinction between soldier and civilian." And second, they "defy the rules of 'fair play' by attempting to gain the advantages of both statuses."[75] In effect, terrorists take on "civilian disguise" like spies and saboteurs behind enemy lines. They do not follow the law of war and therefore are not to be granted its protection.[76] Terrorists violate the very heart of the humanitarian convention by purposely confusing the boundary that separates soldier from civilian, thus putting civilians at risk.

Terrorists ought not be seen as civilian criminals and they themselves reject such a status. Often they see themselves as "freedom fighters" or "guerrilla warriors," but "never claim to be unengaged in combat."[77] Nonetheless, because terrorists do not uphold the rules of warfare they ought not be granted the rights of soldiers. Like soldiers, however, "they may be killed during armed conflict at any time, whether armed or unarmed, whether posing a grievous threat or idly standing by. Unlike regular soldiers, however, they may also be killed in purely civilian settings," for example, in their homes or backyards.[78]

Meisels's approach goes farther than Kretzmer in the wide powers it grants the Israeli state to take life. She maintains that international law needs revision in the way it deals with combatants who do not play by the rules of war. In her view, terrorists as unlawful combatants deserve none of the protections of regular soldiers and certainly none of the rights of lawful civilians.

THE HIGH COURT OF JUSTICE

Within Israel the public debate took a major turn with the promulgation of the opinion of its Supreme Court, sitting as the High Court of Justice, in which the matter of targeted killing was addressed. In 2002 two Israeli human rights groups filed petitions asking that the Israeli Supreme Court ban all targeted killing of Palestinians by the IDF. After an initial delay in addressing the request, the High Court of Justice offered a unanimous opinion written by President Emeritus A. Barak, with President D. Beinisch and Vice President E. Rivlin concurring in the judgment. That decision was handed down on December 13, 2006. The basic conclusion of the court was that even though some incidents of targeted killing may not have been legal, there was insufficient evidence that a total ban on the practice should be implemented.

Key to the judges' reasoning is their starting point: "that between Israel and the various terrorist organizations active in Judea, Samaria, and the Gaza Strip (hereinafter 'the area') a continuous situation of armed conflict has existed since the first *intifada*."[79] The justices acknowledge that the "normative system" that applies to this armed conflict "is complex." Yet at "its center stands the international law regarding international armed conflict." In working through their decision, therefore, the justices relied upon international humanitarian law and where there was a gap in that law it could be supplemented by human rights law as well as Israeli public law.[80]

In a direct reference to David Kretzmer, the judges reject the idea of a "mixed model" that treats the conflict as neither of a "purely national character, but also not of international character," opting instead for a model "of a mixed character, to which both international human rights law and international humanitarian law apply." Instead, the court chose as its starting point the view "that the armed conflict is of an international character."[81] Within that framework the important question regarding status arises once again. What is the status of those engaged in terrorist activity?

To answer that question the court looked at the criteria laid out in both the Hague and the Geneva Conventions. Those four criteria are, as noted earlier: being under a responsible command; wearing a fixed distinctive sign or uniform; carrying weapons openly; and abiding by the laws and customs of war, which, among other things, prohibit the targeting of civilians. Terrorists do not fulfill those conditions and, therefore, the court determined that they "do not fall into the category of combatants."[82]

The only alternative to that status in the international law of warfare is that of civilian. The law defines civilians negatively; they are the opposite of combatants, people who are not members of the armed forces. So in the view of the court, unlawful combatants, those who are engaged in hostilities but who fail the fourfold standard for combatant status, are not combatants at all but civilians. "Does that mean that the unlawful combatants are entitled to the same protection to which civilians who are not unlawful combatants are entitled? The answer is, no." The justices maintain that the customary law of armed conflict is clear that "a civilian taking a direct part in the hostilities does not, at such time, enjoy the protection granted to a civilian who is not taking a direct part in the hostilities." The bottom line for the court is (1) an unlawful combatant is a civilian; (2) however, he is not a civilian protected from attack while he is directly participating in hostilities; (3) civilians who are unlawful combatants may be considered legitimate targets for attack.[83]

Consequently, the "basic principle" that the justices laid down was "civilians taking a direct part in hostilities are not protected at such time they are doing so."[84] In this they follow §51 (3) of the First Protocol of the Geneva Conventions, which the justices understand to be customary international humanitarian law.[85] The court maintains that a civilian who directly participates in hostilities does not lose civilian status, "but as long as he is taking a direct part in hostilities he does not enjoy—during that time—the protection granted to a civilian." A person in that situation is "subject to the risks of attack like those to which a combatant is subject, without enjoying the rights of a combatant."[86]

In order to properly interpret the court's basic principle there are three parts to the principle that require clarification. "The first part is the requirement that civilians take part in 'hostilities'; the second part is the requirement that civilians take a 'direct' part in hostilities; the third part is the provision by which civilians are not protected from attack 'for such time' as they take a direct part in hostilities."[87] The justices then examined each of these parts in separate sections of the opinion.

The idea of hostilities is understood to include acts intended to cause damage or injury to armed forces or civilians. One takes part in such activity not only "when using weapons in an armed conflict," but also "while gathering intelligence, or while preparing himself for the hostilities."[88]

The second part of the basic principle to clarify is taking a direct part. Here the justices admit there is no agreed upon meaning of the term "direct," and so "there is no escaping going case by case" trying to narrow the range of disagreement. An overly narrow rendering would restrict the idea to actual "combat and active military operations," while an overly broad approach would extend the meaning "to the entire war effort."[89]

The court offered several examples of what should count as taking a "direct" part in hostilities: someone collecting intelligence on the other side in the conflict; a person transporting unlawful combatants to or from the locale of the hostilities; anyone who operates or supervises or services the weapons that unlawful combatants employ. Conversely, someone selling food or medicine to an unlawful combatant is taking an indirect part, as is a person who offers general strategic analysis or provides financial aid or distributes propaganda supporting unlawful combatants.[90] For the justices, the "'direct' character of the part taken should not be narrowed merely to the person committing the physical act of attack. Those who have sent him, as well, take a 'direct part.' The same goes for the person who decided upon the act, and the person who planned it."[91]

It is the phrase "for such time" in the third part of the court's basic principle that needs elaboration. This introduces a time element to determination of unlawful combatant status. The court noted that, as with the "direct" participation in hostilities, there is no established consensus on the meaning of the expression. Again, the approach is to use a case-by-case method that tries to narrow down the range of disagreement.

One extreme is the person who takes part in hostilities on a single occasion and then distances himself from that activity going forward. That person ought to be considered a civilian with protection from attack at the moment he distanced himself from the terror activity. As a civilian he should not be targeted for his action in the past. The other extreme is a civilian who joins a terrorist organization that becomes his "home" and that through "his role in that organization he commits a chain of hostilities, with short periods of rest between them." An individual fitting that description "loses his immunity from attack 'for such time' as he is committing the chain of acts." In effect, the "rest between hostilities is nothing other than preparation for the next hostility."[92]

It is between those two extremes that there are gray areas. The court makes four claims. First, the burden of proof lies heavily on those who would attack a civilian that the person is a legitimate target. Second, the determination to perform a targeted killing must not be taken if a less harmful measure is available. Third, there should be a thorough independent investigation done retroactively to determine if the target was legitimately attacked. Fourth, "in appropriate cases it is appropriate to pay compensation as result of harm caused to an innocent civilian."[93]

The court adds a word of caution regarding proportionality, which "applies in every case in which civilians are harmed at such time as they are not taking a direct part in hostilities." The justices accept the proposition that even a legitimate target should not be targeted if the collateral damage of civilian casualties would be "disproportionate to the specific military gain" resulting from the targeted killing.[94]

Although not greeted with universal acclaim by all the disputants in the Israeli debate, the decision of the High Court of Justice has been widely cited as a carefully articulated rationale for why targeted killing can be an acceptable element in a counterterrorism strategy. The justices also delineated the limitations and conditions that should be placed upon any Israeli policy of targeted killing.

TAKEAWAYS FROM THE ISRAELI EXPERIENCE

Before closing this chapter it will be helpful to recall the two sets of bullet points made earlier about the evolution of the Israeli debate over targeted killing. If we consider them along with the later contributions made by the High Court and other commentators, we can draw up a number of issues that grew in clarity as well as those topics that remained confused or under dispute.

First, it would seem that a majority of commentators found the appeal of the law enforcement paradigm as the proper context for assessing targeted killing to be weak. When a host state is either unable or unwilling to cooperate with the victimized state in the identification and arrest of those committing terrorist acts, then the law enforcement approach to counterterrorism is unrealistic. David, Statman, Gross, Guiora, Kretzmer, Meisels, and the High Court all display doubts about the law enforcement model. For the majority of commentators it was evident that the terror attacks during the height of the second Intifada were not sporadic and isolated but organized, systematic, and occurred with regularity. There was a widely felt sense that the terrorist campaign posed a serious threat to the lives and security of innocent Israeli civilians and that the Israeli state had a duty to defend the lives of its citizens. Declaring Israel to be in a state of armed conflict was a plausible description of the situation.

Second, in the armed conflict paradigm the criteria for moral assessment of Israel's policy should be drawn from the just war tradition. Criteria drawn from that moral tradition continue to provide important guidance to judgments about targeted killing in counterterrorist campaigns. And as Statman, Gross, Guiora, and others point out, those criteria require more than establishment of self-defense as a just cause. There must be attention to other moral norms such as last resort or necessity, utility or a reasonable hope of success, and proportionality or minimalizing collateral damage. It is because of such concern for the fuller range of just war criteria that most authors do not support the suggestion of Yadlin and Kasher that the safety of IDF personnel has priority over that of Palestinian civilians. Concern for just war norms also leads to the High Court's reservations about Meisels's proposal that terrorists deserve none of the protections accorded to lawful combatants.

Third, it remains a matter of open debate whether international humanitarian law, which governs armed conflict, adequately addresses the status of those involved in international terrorism. Certainly those engaged in terrorist attacks are not lawful combatants. And there is equal clarity that the "revolving door" approach to terrorists changing status quickly once they are not actually engaged in an attack defies common sense. There is also a lack of clarity regarding the status of those civilians involved in a variety of roles in the chain of causality who enable terrorist attacks upon Israeli citizens. Nonetheless, as Statman and the High Court persuasively argue, the list of those subject to targeting extends beyond the actual attacker to include some of the actors playing other roles in the causal chain. As the court suggested, determining which actors play a role may require a case-by-case investigation.

Fourth, there is an acknowledgment that the effectiveness of a policy of targeted killing is best judged by its cumulative effect in undermining or destroying the ability of terrorists to launch successful attacks upon Israeli civilians. Luft, David, and Statman have all supported this idea. The targeted killing policy did have an impact in lessening the frequency and lethality of terrorist attacks. That is demonstrable. Should that, however, be the sole measure of success or are there broader policy aims that must be considered? And what weight ought targeted killing be given when balanced with advancement of the peace process? These are fair questions. Without doubt there has been a political and diplomatic price to pay for the targeted killing policy. Certainly the policy has made it far more difficult for moderates within the Palestinian community to get a hearing when offering nonviolent alternatives to the terrorist option.

Fifth, the decision to approve a targeted killing requires assignment of individual responsibility for the wrongdoing of terrorist action. There remains debate over the idea of putting a person on a target list simply on the basis of membership in organizations that sponsor terrorism. Gross has suggested that a thorough process of vetting candidates for a target list will itself be the way to determine if a given individual should be made an object of targeted killing. Such a process will clarify the actual status of a person better than a priori judgments about membership. The admitted errors in some targeted killings—misidentifications of the target and errors in judgment about proportionality leading to unacceptable civilian deaths—led the High Court of Justice to assert the need for independent judicial review of targeted killings to be done retroactively. This was determined to be necessary since the decision to target a civilian for killing must be justified on grounds that the person posed a real and imminent threat to the lives of innocent civilians or IDF members and then that the targeted killing must be carried out properly. The court maintained that judgment and assessment of a targeted killing ought not be solely in the power of the executive or military leadership.

Sixth, targeted killing should be used only for necessary defense against a serious terrorist threat. Its role is that of preemption, not retribution or revenge. Despite the claim of one intelligence officer that the victims of Operation Wrath of God were actually involved in plans for future attacks, it seems that the Israeli actions might have been more akin to extrajudicial execution than targeted killing.[95] And there have been other instances where retribution rather than preemption seems to have been the dominant motive.[96]

In July 2001, Richard Boucher, a spokesman for the U.S. State Department, stated, "Targeted killings of Palestinians don't end the violence but are only inflaming an already volatile situation." A few months later, after the terrorist attacks of September 11, he stated that "the U.S. embrace of targeted killings would silence this criticism from Israel's most important ally."[97] Then with the onset of armed drone use as a central element in U.S. counterterrorism strategy, the discussion of targeted killing took a new turn. The Bush administration initiated the practice of drone attacks, but it was the Obama administration that ratcheted up the use of drones to a new level. Much of the vocabulary and many of the problems and viewpoints that we have seen in our examination of the distant and proximate contexts will return now in the immediate context of U.S. drone policy. In the next chapter we will examine the policy and practice of armed drone use in the counterterrorism strategy of the United States.

4

THE IMMEDIATE CONTEXT

The U.S. War on Terrorism

The direct, targeted killing of particular individuals is now a prominent feature of the counterterrorism strategy followed by the United States. Any review of the literature quickly reveals there are many who harbor reservations about the strategy as well as others who oppose it outright. Yet there are a good number of people who defend targeted killing not only as strategically necessary, but also as morally preferable to the killing that occurs in a conventional war.

It is evident that the norm against targeted killing, which had been fairly strong during the past three centuries, is now in something of a decline. While various elements factor into the reason for the decline, it is certain that the rise of guerrilla warfare, terrorist acts, irregular armed combatants, and other characteristics of asymmetric warfare have played a role. Even more so, the threat of terrorism has served as a significant rationale for the new reliance upon targeted killing.

In the United States the opposition to targeted killing, once strong, shifted considerably after 9/11. Whereas it once expressed deep opposition to the Israeli policy, the United States is now, in the eyes of many, the foremost practitioner of targeted killing throughout the world. The arguments surrounding this shift are sometimes conflated with another development in U.S. counterterrorism activity, the use of drones. While the two are related because the United States commonly uses attack drones to carry out targeted killings, they are not the same. Thus, reasons to oppose one practice may not be as telling against the other.

Another element in the U.S. discussion about drones and targeted killing is the lack of transparency about the government's policy. Criticisms of the U.S. policy are often aimed at the Obama administration's reluctance to be forthcoming about details of its policy and its implementation. Thus, it is useful to present background information on the U.S. doctrine and practice in this chapter before examining the criticisms of the Obama administration's policy in chapter 5.

THE OBAMA ADMINISTRATION'S POLICY

On December 10, 2009, Barack Obama received the Nobel Peace Prize in Oslo, Norway. In his acceptance speech he told his audience the "hard truth": "We will not eradicate violent conflict in our lifetimes. There will be times when nations—acting individually or in concert—will find the use of force not only necessary but morally justified."[1] The president went on to say that when the use of armed force is necessary "and even as we confront a vicious adversary that abides by no rules, I believe the United States of America must remain a standard bearer in the conduct of war."[2]

The president's speech was generally well received, but some critics on the political left found the claim that the United States was "a standard bearer in the conduct of war" to be undercut by the Obama administration's use of targeted killing. When running for office Obama attacked the Bush administration for its use of torture, for the detainee program at Guantanamo Bay, and for the decline in the international reputation of the nation as a result of the Bush administration's prosecution of its war on terrorism. And yet by the time Obama spoke in Oslo, less than a year into his presidency, he had already personally authorized more drone strikes than George Bush had in his entire presidency.[3]

Had people followed Obama's campaign rhetoric closely, his use of attack drones ought not have been a shock. In August 2007 he stated, "I will not hesitate to use force to take out terrorists who pose a direct threat to America. I will ensure that the military becomes more stealthy, agile, and lethal in its ability to capture or kill terrorists."[4] Then in remarks he made in May 2009, the president observed that the government needed "new tools to protect the American people, and that these tools would have to allow us to prevent attacks instead of simply prosecuting those who carry them out."[5]

Obama's attitude toward targeted killing and drones was taking shape prior to his entering the White House. An informative book about the president's thinking on counterterrorism recounts that on November 6, 2008, two days after his election, Obama met with Vice Admiral Mike McConnell in Chicago to receive his first intelligence briefing as the president-elect. During the meeting McConnell gave Obama information about "the inner workings of the CIA's covert drone program," including the successful destruction of much of al-Qaida's top leadership.[6]

Just a few days later the president-elect interviewed John Brennan as part of the search process for a CIA director. Both men agreed on the necessity for a counterterrorism strategy that reached down to the roots of terrorism, the alienation of many Arab youth living in politically authoritarian societies where there was poverty and little upward mobility. At the same time, Obama and Brennan agreed on the need for a more surgical strategy, focused on clear threats to the United States. "It was like attacking a spreading cancer, Brennan told the pres-elect: 'You need to target the metastasizing disease without destroying the surrounding tissue.'" With regard to the tactics of how to do that, Obama related what he had learned about the drone program, which soon became "the new administration's weapon of choice."[7]

After the inauguration the CIA drone program continued to operate under the same rules of target selection, secrecy, and operational procedures established by the Bush administration. On January 23, a drone strike occurred in the village of Karez Kot, within the federally administered tribal areas of Pakistan. The intended target was a group of suspected militants in a house. However, the actual house that was hit belonged to a tribal elder who was supportive of the Pakistan government and who had been engaged in peacebuilding efforts. He and four family members, including two children, were killed. Shortly after the news of the deadly error the new president quizzed the CIA director, Michael Hayden, on what went wrong and why. During the meeting Obama learned for the first time about the difference between signature and high-value strikes. Signature strikes are attacks launched against a target whose identity is not determined yet who is believed to be a terrorist due to certain suspicious behavior. High-value strikes, on the other hand, are those aimed at known individuals who play a significant role in a terrorist organization. The president expressed unhappiness with the idea of signature strikes due to the danger of targeting innocents, but when the meeting ended the CIA practice remained in place. Signature strikes would continue and the decision to approve a strike remained within the CIA.[8]

As the president had come to learn, the drone program of targeted killing was unquestionably a tactical success in killing al-Qaida leaders and even its midlevel personnel. However, its role in bringing about the strategic success of ending terror was less clear. Obama knew there were limits to what targeted killing could do. "But Obama believed he had to stay focused not only on the big picture but also on the individual terrorist who might slip US defenses and attack the homeland."[9] So although he knew attack drones could not bring about the strategic aim of winning the war on terror, Obama was appreciative of their effectiveness in stopping terrorists from killing Americans.

Human rights groups were critical of the resort to targeted killing and the use of drones. Indeed, the UN rapporteur suggested that the practice of targeted killing using drones might involve war crimes. Not only the wisdom but also the legality of the administration's policy was questioned. Nonetheless, Obama was kept closely informed about the CIA program by Leon Panetta, who replaced Hayden as director of the agency. The president, according to reports, was impressed with the care taken in identifying targets and determining when to strike.[10]

A PUBLIC KILLING

Anwar al-Awlaki, a Muslim cleric and a native-born American citizen, died in northern Yemen in the fall of 2011. He had been specifically targeted in a CIA drone attack. Awlaki was born in Las Cruces, New Mexico, while his Yemeni father was on a Fulbright grant studying at New Mexico State University. The son lived in the United States until he was eleven years old before the family moved back to Yemen. He returned to attend college in 1991.

Awlaki was an active leader of al-Qaida in the Arabian Peninsula (AQAP). As someone who was actively engaged in plotting terrorist acts against the United States it was inconsequential to the Obama administration that Awlaki was a U.S. citizen. Yet upon his death there was a significant outcry about the government killing an American citizen without benefit of due process of law as guaranteed by the U.S. Constitution. A key clause in the Fifth Amendment to the Constitution secures the fundamental right that no citizen should be "deprived of life, liberty, or property, without due process of law," that is, without the opportunity to contest the prosecution's evidence in a court of law.

As far back as December 2009, Obama had concluded that Awlaki "posed a serious and imminent threat to the security of the American people. That he was an American, Obama believed, was immaterial."[11] In June 2010 the Justice Department issued a secret opinion authorizing a targeted killing of Awlaki, if capture was not feasible. There was little doubt from the intelligence reports that Awlaki wanted to strike at his native land.

Contrary to some public characterizations, Awlaki was not just a religious preacher or effective online recruiter to AQAP. He was also an active planner and strategist for terror strikes. He had become the chief of external operations for AQAP. Awlaki was involved with the failed Christmas Day 2009 plot to blow up an American airliner; he hatched the 2010 plan to place bombs in toner cartridges being shipped to the United States for Hewlett-Packard printers; and then in the summer of 2011 there was the news that surgically implanted bombs in suicide bombers capable of avoiding airport body scanners had already worked with dogs and other animals.[12] "What worried Obama most was Awlaki's relentlessness and ingenuity in developing murderous plots that could get around America's best defenses."[13]

Based on the Freedom of Information Act, the *New York Times* and the American Civil Liberties Union jointly filed a lawsuit seeking release of the June 2010 memo that determined a drone attack on Awlaki would be legal. The administration resisted the request. However, in January 2013 a white paper that summarized the Justice Department document was leaked to a reporter for NBC News. It was made public and evoked an intense response from critics.

The document was a sixteen-page summary of the classified Justice Department memo and had been prepared for members of the Senate Intelligence and Judiciary Committees. It had been sent to them in June 2012 on the condition that it be kept confidential. Although not an official legal memo, the white paper was prepared by Justice Department lawyers and the congressional recipients were told that it accurately reflected the arguments of the classified memos on targeted killing that the Office of Legal Counsel in the Justice Department gave the executive branch as authoritative legal guidance.[14]

The unsigned memo was narrowly focused, addressing only "the circumstances in which the U.S. government could use lethal force in a foreign country outside the area of active hostilities against a US citizen who is a senior operational leader of al-Qaida or an associated force of al-Qaida—that is an al-Qaida leader actively engaged in planning operations to kill Americans."[15] The memo cites three conditions under which such a lethal operation could be legal:

1. "an informed, high-level official of the U.S. government has determined that the targeted individual poses an imminent threat of violent attack against the United States";
2. "capture is infeasible, and the United States continues to monitor whether capture becomes feasible";
3. "the operation would be conducted in a manner consistent with applicable law of war principles."[16]

The document then analyzed how its conclusion stands up against four different possible legal objections: that such a targeted killing violates the Fifth Amendment guarantee of due process; that such a targeted killing violates the Fourth Amendment's prohibition on unreasonable seizures; that such a targeted killing violates criminal laws prohibiting the killing of US nationals abroad; and that such a targeted killing violates the prohibition against assassination in Executive Order 12333. Taking each argument in turn, the memo concluded the specific case of a targeted killing under consideration is permissible if the three conditions enumerated above exist.

Criticism of the memo's reasoning was extensive and immediate. An illustration of the typical criticisms may be found in an essay by Rosa Brooks.[17]

1. It is true that American citizens can be targeted and killed by the United States if they take up arms against the United States. That is uncontroversial under the law of war. An American who joined the Nazi army during World War II could be killed like any other German soldier. The problem is that the present conflict is unlike World War II. There are major disagreements over what it means to be a combatant or to be a participant in hostilities. The memo never defines who the "senior operational leaders of al-Qaida and its associated forces" are. How many are there? And what is an "associated force"?
2. The memo maintains that a citizen who poses an "imminent threat of violent attack" may be legitimately targeted. That is not controversial as a statement of self-defense but it is far too vague. What is meant by "imminent" threat? Traditionally, the term is understood narrowly within legal literature. A threat cannot be distant or speculative. However, that is precisely what the Justice Department seems to mean by its use of the term. The memo states that imminence "does not require the United States to have clear evidence that a specific attack on U.S. persons and interests will take place in the immediate future." The memo conflates the idea of immi-

nence with identity. If you are an "operational leader" of al-Qaida or its associated forces you are by definition an imminent threat.

3. A targeted killing is permissible when capture is not feasible. That, too, has initial plausibility, but what is meant by feasible? What level of risk ought the military or other government agents assume before deciding they can kill an American citizen with no opportunity to present evidence that he has been mistakenly targeted? Who makes the judgment call that capture is not feasible?
4. The decision to employ a targeted killing against an American citizen is made by "an informed, high-level official of the U.S. government." Is that the president or vice president? The head of the CIA? The secretary of defense? An air force colonel? What is the chain of command? Is the decision to be made by one official? What if other officials disagree? What if the high-level individual is misinformed? What are the safeguards against abuse or poor decisions?
5. The last question leads to the next criticism. The white paper states simply that "there exists no appropriate judicial forum to evaluate these constitutional questions." As Brooks put it, "the standards put forth in the memo are effectively standardless."[18] There is no mention of a review mechanism, of any system of checks and balances that involves someone from outside the executive branch. There is no clarity about whether there is even within the executive branch someone who plays the role of devil's advocate before putting a person on the kill list.[19]

Another common criticism made about the Obama administration's policy was the secrecy and lack of transparency. At the time the white paper was leaked the White House had not even acknowledged it was the United States that had killed Anwar al-Awlaki fifteen months earlier. In his State of the Union address on February 12, 2013, the president made a pledge of greater transparency concerning the policy of targeted killing and the use of drones. Nonetheless, many thought the pledge was not being taken seriously by the administration.[20]

A PUBLIC HEARING

Public knowledge of the white paper and of the existence of undisclosed Justice Department memos fed into a second incident that pushed debate over the U.S. policy into the public forum. On January 7, 2013, the president nominated John Brennan, the architect of the drone program while serving as the administration's chief advisor on counterterrorism, to be the director of the CIA, replacing Leon Panetta. The nomination required the approval of the Senate Intelligence Committee and the full Senate. Before the Intelligence Committee would vote on his nomination Brennan had to appear in person to give testimony and answer senators' questions. It would be the first time that a high-level administration official would have to answer questions about targeted killing and the use of drones. A bipartisan group of senators also saw the nomination as a way to press the White House to release official documents, particularly the June 2010 memo. A conviction shared by both Republicans and Democrats was that Congress was being denied the information it needed to perform its oversight role. The Brennan nomination gave the Senate "an ideal opportunity to demand that the White House be more forthcoming."[21]

The White House did report on a routine basis to both the Senate and House Intelligence and Armed Service Committees regarding drone attacks. However, it also routinely denied congressional efforts to access the legal opinions that authorized those strikes. Until the pending Senate nomination hearing, the only document available was the white paper summary of the actual memos. Even when the Justice Department documents were finally shared it was for a limited time and only to senators, not staff lawyers or security experts.[22]

In addition to the classified session there was a public hearing, although the topic of drones did not get as much attention as some thought it deserved. Brennan was asked by several senators to discuss transparency and cooperation with the congressional role of oversight. He also was asked questions about leaks, CIA detention and torture, and the incident of the attack on the U.S. embassy in Benghazi, Libya. Senators Wyden (D-OR), King (I-ME), and Collins (R-ME) were the three members of the committee who most directly interrogated the nominee on drones and targeted killing.[23]

In his oral answers during the public hearing and in written responses to prehearing questions submitted by the committee, Brennan made several points. He agreed with Wyden that the American public needed to have a better understanding of the rules and processes the government follows when determining that an armed drone is to be used in a targeted killing. "So what we need to do is make sure we explain to the American people what *are* the thresholds for action, what *are* the procedures, the practices, the processes, the approvals, the reviews."[24] He also told the committee that a targeted killing was used only as a last resort to protect American lives and the United States does not conduct strikes "to punish terrorists for past transgressions" but to prevent future terrorist acts.[25]

In response to a question about how the government determines when an individual or group is "associated" with al-Qaida, Brennan clarified the meaning of "associated force" as used in the Justice Department white paper. He stated that there are two characteristics that characterize an associated force: "(1) an organized, armed group that entered the fight alongside al-Qaida, and (2) a co-belligerent with al-Qaida in hostilities against the United States or its coalition partners."[26]

Brennan also expressed regret that the public did not realize "the care we take and the agony that we go through to make sure that we do not have any collateral injuries or deaths."[27] He stated that civilian deaths are "much, much rarer than many allege."[28]

What the hearing and testimony revealed to the public was that there was indeed an organized process and protocols to follow in the use of targeted killing and drone attacks. What the hearing and testimony did not reveal was any specific information about what the process and protocols were, who was involved, and how one moved through the process.

At several points in his remarks as well as in the questions posed, references were made to public, nonclassified speeches that administration figures had given on the policy of targeted killing and the use of drones. Those speeches, which did not get as much attention as they deserved when given, were cited by senators and Brennan as important windows into what for many was a dark room.

SPEAKING IN PUBLIC

When the Justice Department's white paper was leaked, a spokeswoman for the department, Tracy Schmaler, refused to answer any questions about the document but "pointed to public speeches by what she called a 'parade' of administration officials, including Brennan, [Attorney General Eric] Holder, former State Department legal advisor Harold Koh, and former Defense Department general counsel Jeh Johnson that she said outlined the 'legal framework' for such operations."[29] And when he was asked for additional information on administration policy, Jay Carney, the White House spokesman, "suggested that reporters should be satisfied with the now-leaked white paper, in addition to speeches by administration officials."[30] Those speeches constitute an important source for understanding the Obama administration's policy.

Harold Koh

The first major speech on targeted killing by a key administration figure came from an unlikely person, Harold Koh, a Yale law professor on leave while serving as chief legal advisor to the Department of State. Koh was a respected legal scholar and enjoyed a good reputation among human rights groups. In his role at State, Koh traveled widely and found himself hearing a lot of complaints from European officials and international lawyers about the drone program. He also was hearing similar comments from human rights groups back in the United States. As a loyal member of the foreign policy team, Koh defended the U.S. drone policy's legal status. Yet he became worried that because the drone program was covert the administration was not making a persuasive case in explaining the program to allies and the domestic public. He lobbied to make a speech defending what the United States was doing, and on March 25, 2012, Koh gave a speech in which he argued the legality of both the drone program and targeted killing to the Annual Meeting of the American Society of International Law.

After noting that al-Qaida and its associated forces do not fight as a conventional army, Koh commented upon the idea of targeted killing. First, he observed that whether a person is targeted in a particular location must be determined on a case-by-case basis, weighing "considerations specific to each case, including those related to the imminence of the threat, the sovereignty of the other states involved, and the willingness and ability of those states to suppress the threat the target poses." Koh then assured the audience that the Obama administration "has carefully reviewed the rules governing targeting operations to ensure that these operations are conducted consistently with law of war principles" so that "only legitimate objectives are targeted and that collateral damage is kept to a minimum."[31]

While not responding in detail to objections to the Obama policy, Koh did respond to four commonly raised complaints. To those who suggest that targeting specific leaders violates the laws of war, he asserted that "individuals who are part of such an armed group are belligerents and, therefore, lawful targets under international law." Others have questioned the use of unmanned aerial vehicles in lethal operations, "but the rules that govern targeting do not turn on the type of weapon system used, and there is no prohibition under the laws of war on the use of technologically advanced weapons systems in armed conflict . . . so long as they are employed in conformity with applicable laws of war." In response to the charge that targeted killing "constitutes unlawful extrajudicial killing," Koh argued that "a state that is engaged in an armed conflict or in legitimate self-defense is not required to provide targets with legal process before the state may use force." And finally, Koh rebutted those who claim targeted killing violates the U.S. domestic ban on assassinations. "[U]nder domestic law, the use of lawful weapons systems—consistent with the applicable laws of war—for precision targeting of specific high-level belligerent leaders when acting in self-defense or during an armed conflict is not unlawful, and hence does not constitute 'assassination.'"[32]

After his speech Koh continued to reflect upon the targeting policy of the administration and eventually developed his own four-part test for determining the legality of killing away from a recognized battlefield:

1. The target is clearly part of al-Qaida or an associated force.
2. The target has to be a senior member of the terrorist group and this is determined by weighing uniqueness versus fungibility. If the target could be easily replaced there is no unique threat.
3. The target has to be "externally focused," meaning, not caught up in local politics but desiring to attack America.
4. There is evidence the target is plotting to strike.[33]

Koh also developed the idea of "elongated imminence" that he likened to "battered spouse syndrome" whereby a spouse does not have to wait till a hand is being raised to strike before acting in self-defense if there is a pattern of past abuse.[34]

John Brennan (I)

There were four other public speeches given by administration officials after Koh's remarks in March 2010 and prior to Brennan's Senate testimony in February 2013. About eighteen months after Koh delivered his speech, John Brennan, speaking as Obama's then chief aide for counterterrorism, spoke at Harvard Law School. In comments about the "guiding principles" that inform the administration's policy Brennan stated that adhering to the rule of law is a principle that is followed in "all our actions, foreign and domestic" and "that includes covert actions, which we undertake under the authorities provided to us by Congress."[35]

In a speech that touched upon a number of topics, Brennan made two points of particular significance for the targeted killing policy and drone program. With regard to the geographic scope of the conflict with al-Qaida, the United States "does not view our authority to use military force against al-Qaida as being restricted solely to 'hot' battlefields like Afghanistan. . . . [T]he United States takes the legal position that—in accordance with international law—we have the authority to take action against al-Qa'ida and its associated forces without doing a separate self-defense analysis each time." Further, "we reserve the right to take unilateral action if or when other governments are unwilling or unable to take the necessary actions themselves" to prevent al-Qaida or its associated forces from attacking us.[36]

The other significant point made in the speech involved the issue of "imminence" when assessing the nature of the threat posed. Brennan claimed that there was "increasing recognition in the international community that a more flexible understanding of 'imminence' may be appropriate when dealing with terrorist groups," because the threats posed by nonstate actors are so different than in more traditional interstate conflicts. "After all, al-Qaida does not follow a traditional command structure, wear uniforms, carry its arms openly, or mass its troops at the borders of the nations it attacks. Nonetheless, it possesses the demonstrated capability to strike with little notice and cause significant civilian or military casualties."[37]

Jeh Johnson

Early in the next year, on February 22, 2012, Jeh Johnson, general counsel for the Department of Defense, gave a speech at Yale Law School that further elucidated the thinking of the Obama administration on the conflict with al-Qaida. Johnson made clear that "the bedrock of the military's domestic legal authority continues to be the Authorization for the Use of Military Force (AUMF) passed by Congress one week after 9/11." In that legislation the president was authorized to "use all necessary and appropriate force against those nations, organizations, or persons he determines planned, authorized, committed, or aided the terrorist attacks that occurred on September 11, 2001, or harbored such organizations or persons, in order to prevent any future acts of international terrorism against the United States by such nations, organizations or persons."[38]

In an important clarification, Johnson explained that the idea of an "associated force" is not an open-ended one. "It does not authorize military force against anyone the Executive labels a 'terrorist.'" Yet, with the decentralization of al-Qaida, the relevance of associated forces is undeniable as the original organization "relies more on associates to carry out its terrorist aims." Johnson established two characteristics of an associated force. First, it is "an organized, armed group that has entered the fight alongside al-Qaida," and second, it "is a co-belligerent with al-Qaida in hostilities against the United States or its coalition partners. In other words, the group must not only be aligned with al-Qaida." Rather, to be an associated force the group "must also have entered the fight against the United States or its coalition partners. Thus, an 'associated force' is not any terrorist group in the world that merely embraces the al-Qaida ideology."[39] That understanding of an associated force would also be found in Brennan's written response to the Senate Intelligence Committee's questions in 2013.

Johnson also took up one of the key points Brennan had made at Harvard, that "there is nothing in the wording of the 2001 AUMF or its legislative history that restricts this statutory authority to the 'hot' battlefields of Afghanistan." The AUMF gave the president the authority to use "necessary and appropriate force against the organizations and persons connected to the September 11th attacks—al-Qaida and the Taliban—without a geographic limitation." Because al-Qaida has decentralized and migrated from Afghanistan in search of new safe havens, the geographic spread of the conflict is understandable. Yet there are limits, for the Obama administration does not "believe we are in any 'Global War on Terror,' or that we can use military force whenever we want, wherever we want." The principles of international law, including state sovereignty and the laws of war, restrain unilateral action and the use of force in other nations.[40]

Johnson also picked up on Koh's speech from 2010 in which he defended the practice of targeted killing. He observed that during a state of armed conflict, to employ "lethal force against known, individual members of the enemy is a long-standing and long-legal practice." Johnson then acknowledged, "[W]hat is new is that, with advances in technology, we are able to target military objectives with much more precision, to the point where we can identify, target and strike a single military objective from great distances." Yet the rules governing targeting under the laws of war "do not turn on the type of weapon system used, and there is no prohibition under the law of war on the use of technologically advanced weapons systems." Indeed, such advances may minimize civilian casualties. Johnson then dismissed the charge that targeted killing is really the same as assassination. "Under well-settled legal principles, lethal force against a valid *military* objective, in an armed conflict, is consistent with the law of war and does not, by definition, constitute an 'assassination.'"[41]

Eric Holder

Less than two weeks after Johnson's lecture at Yale, Attorney General Eric Holder spoke at the School of Law at Northwestern University. He, too, addressed the legal basis for the United States to use force abroad, citing the constitutional obligation of the president to defend the nation, the AUMF passed by Congress, the right of national self-defense under international law, as well as the inherent right to defend against an imminent threat of attack. For Holder, "none of this is changed by the fact that we are not in a conventional war."[42]

The attorney general also agreed that the administration's legal mandate was not limited to Afghanistan, noting that "neither Congress nor our federal courts has limited the geographic scope of our ability to use force" solely to Afghanistan. "We are at war with a stateless enemy, prone to shifting operations from country to country." Holder told his audience that since he assumed office, several attacks unsuccessfully directed at the United States stemmed from countries other than Afghanistan. The government has a duty to protect the nation from such threats. According to Holder, and as had been stated by others, this does not mean there are no restraints upon U.S. military action abroad. There is an obligation to respect sovereignty and to avoid unilateral action. "But the use of force in a foreign territory would be consistent with these international legal principles if conducted, for example, with the consent of the nation involved—or after a determination that the nation is unable or unwilling to deal effectively with a threat to the United States."[43]

Like his colleagues Koh and Johnson, Holder also explained that a targeted killing is not an assassination. The latter is unlawful. However, "the U.S. government's use of lethal force in self-defense against a leader of al-Qaida or an associated force who presents an imminent threat of violent attack would not be unlawful" and thus, it would not violate the executive order banning assassination.[44]

Holder also commented upon the concept of an "imminent threat" and suggested that when assessing whether a given individual poses an imminent threat there must be consideration of "the relevant window of opportunity to act, the possible harm that missing the window would cause to civilians, and the likelihood of heading off future disastrous attacks against the United States." Given the ability of contemporary terrorists to strike with little or no advance warning means the president cannot delay action till "the precise time, place, and manner of attack becomes clear." It is enough to know the individual is an active leader in al-Qaida or an associated force who is "continually planning attacks against the United States."[45]

According to Holder, if capture and detention are not feasible the use of lethal force may be permissible. Of course, any such use of lethal force must comply with the fundamental law of war principles governing the use of force—necessity, distinction, proportionality, and humanity.[46] The principle of necessity requires that the target have definite military value. The principle of distinction requires that only lawful targets—such as combatants, civilians directly participating in hostilities, and military objectives—may be targeted intentionally. Under the principle of proportionality, the anticipated collateral damage must not be excessive in relation to the anticipated military advantage. Finally, the principle of humanity requires the use of weapons that will not inflict unnecessary suffering.

John Brennan (2)

In what had seemingly become a monthly event in early 2012, John Brennan (in his second speech) became the third top-level administration official to speak about the administration's counterterrorism strategy in April. After a review of the status of al-Qaida in which Brennan asserted the organization was damaged and in decline yet still dangerous, he turned his attention to what the United States did to bring about the situation. "So let me say it as simply as I can. Yes, in full accordance with the law, and in order to prevent terrorist attacks on the United States and to save American lives, the United States Government conducts targeted strikes against specific al-Qaida terrorists, sometimes using remotely piloted aircraft, often referred to publicly as drones."[47] The general acknowledgment of the practice of targeted killing using drones was news, but the administration was not admitting any particular act of targeted killing via drone attack, including the killing of Anwar al-Awlaki.

Brennan then appealed to the varieties of law—constitutional, congressional, international—that authorized the use of drone strikes in targeted killing and made the US policy licit. He cited the speeches of Koh, Johnson, and Holder to bolster his viewpoint. Brennan then discussed the ethics of targeted killing and appealed to the "basic principles of the law of war" to make his case.[48]

The use of drones in targeted strikes conforms to the principle of necessity, "the requirement that the target have definite military value." Those "individuals who are part of al-Qaida or its associate forces are legitimate military targets." The U.S.-sponsored strikes satisfy the principle of distinction, "the idea that only military objectives may be intentionally targeted and that civilians are protected from being intentionally targeted." In fact, Brennan stated, "one could argue that never before has there been a weapon that allows us to distinguish more effectively between an al-Qaida terrorist and innocent civilians." Third, the targeted strikes also conform to the principle of proportionality, "the notion that the anticipated collateral damage of an action cannot be excessive in relation to the anticipated military advantage." The ability to specifically target a particular terrorist or small group of terrorists with a bomb that can be manipulated to avoid harming others in the vicinity makes it "hard to imagine a tool that can better minimize the risk to civilians than remotely piloted aircraft." Finally, such strikes satisfy the principle of humanity that requires the use of "weapons that will not inflict unnecessary suffering." Brennan concluded his ethical case, "[F]or all these reasons, I suggest to you that these targeted strikes against al-Qaida terrorists are indeed ethical and just."[49]

He then turned his attention to the question of the wisdom of such strikes, their advisability and appropriateness in a particular circumstance. Brennan argued the drone strikes are a wise choice for a variety of reasons. One set of reasons has to do with geography, as these vehicles have the "ability to fly hundreds of miles over the most treacherous terrain" in regions not easily reached by land forces. There is also the issue of timing, because "windows of opportunity can close quickly and there may be just minutes to act." Importantly, the drone strikes are a wise choice "because they dramatically reduce the danger to U.S. personnel, even eliminating the danger altogether." As well, they "dramatically reduce the danger to innocent civilians," especially when compared to other forms of bombardment. There is a "surgical precision" to drone strikes, "the ability with laser-like focus, to eliminate the cancerous tumor called an al-Qaida terrorist while limiting the damage to the tissue around it." And there is a strategic wisdom to the use of drones for there are "consequences that inevitably come with the use of force. The deployment of large armies abroad, placing armed foreigners in the cities and villages of countries, arouses feelings that "inflame anti-American resentment and inspire the next generation of terrorists."[50]

Having defended the effectiveness, legality, morality, and wisdom of the use of drones in targeted killing, Brennan acknowledged that "we—as a government—along with our foreign partners, can and must do a better job of addressing the mistaken belief among some foreign publics that we engage in these strikes casually, as if we are simply unwilling to expose U.S. forces to the dangers faced every day by people in those regions."[51] Brennan then continued his remarks by elaborating upon the process used in determining whether to launch a targeted killing strike. In doing that he provided more insight into the policy than had previously been shared in the first four years of the Obama presidency.

First, Brennan related that the president and the members of his national security staff "are very mindful that as our nation uses this technology, we are establishing precedents that other nations may follow." Therefore, "if we want other nations to use these technologies responsibly, we must use them responsibly."[52]

Brennan proceeded to discuss the decision to target an individual. First, a counterterrorism professional assesses that a suspected member of al-Qaida poses a threat to the United States and proposes the suspect for consideration. That begins a careful review that will involve "the very most senior officials in our government." At the outset, it must be made clear that a person is a "legitimate target under the law," meaning a person who is "part of al-Qaida, the Taliban, and associated forces." This review "only establishes the outer limits of the authority" under which the counterterrorism policy operates.[53]

Because there are thousands of people who are members of al-Qaida, the Taliban, or associated forces it must be determined "whether [an] individual's activities rise to a certain threshold for action, and whether taking action will, in fact, enhance our security." The "threshold" is that the person poses a "significant threat" to the United States, so lethal action is not taken "in order to eliminate every single member of al-Qaida in the world." Also, Brennan added, lethal action is not "about punishing terrorists for past crimes; we are not seeking vengeance. Rather we conduct targeted strikes because they are necessary to mitigate an actual ongoing threat—to stop plots, prevent future attacks, and save American lives."[54]

A significant threat is not hypothetical; "the mere possibility" that a member of al-Qaida could attack someday is insufficient. A significant threat is "posed by an individual who is an operational leader of al-Qaida or one of its associated forces. Or perhaps the individual is himself an operative, in the midst of actually training for or planning to carry out attacks. . . . Or perhaps the individual possesses unique operational skills that are being leveraged in a planned attack." The goal of targeted killing drone strikes is to disrupt actual plans and real plots "before they come to fruition." However, lethal action is only employed when capture is not feasible. Because capture permits interrogation and intelligence gathering, it is the "unqualified preference" of the administration to "capture suspected terrorists whenever and wherever feasible."[55]

Finally, a strike is only authorized if there is "a high degree of confidence that innocent civilians will not be injured or killed, except in the rarest of circumstances."[56] It is the advanced technology used on drones that permits "greater proximity to the target for a longer period of time," and that, in turn, allows a better grasp of "what is happening in real time on the ground." Consequently, it is possible to "be much more discriminating" and to "make more informed judgments about factors that might contribute to collateral damage."[57]

Without question, Brennan's speech was the most informative for the general public to learn about the process involved in the policy of targeted killing and the role of drones in implementing that policy. No doubt he was aware of criticisms concerning the administration's lack of forthrightness about its policy and wanted to affirm a commitment to transparency. "With that in mind, I have made a sincere effort today to address some of the main questions that citizens and scholars have raised regarding the use of targeted lethal force against al-Qaida."[58]

THE PRESIDENT'S SPEECH

On May 23, 2013, President Obama spoke at the National Defense University, located at Fort McNair in Washington, DC. It was the first speech after his reelection to be devoted to national security matters and it was portrayed in advance as a comprehensive statement of his policy on counterterrorism. The speech was, indeed, comprehensive and touched upon many points, not all of which pertain to the topic of targeted killing and drones. The president spoke for nearly an hour.

Obama began with an overview of what had been accomplished in the fight against terrorism and then laid out what he saw as remaining and newly emerging threats. He also admitted there were limitations in what could be done in counterterrorist activity. Some of the limitations have to do with the places where terrorist groups are located. "In some of these places—such as parts of Somalia and Yemen—the state has only the most tenuous reach into the territory. In other cases, the state lacks the capacity or will to take action." Some of the limitations are military. "It is also not possible for America to simply deploy a team of Special Forces to capture every terrorist." Some limits are due to moral concerns for the potential loss of life. "[T]here are places where it would pose profound risks to our troops and local civilians—where a terrorist compound cannot be breached without triggering a firefight with surrounding tribal communities that pose no threat to us." And there are geopolitical limits as well, "when putting U.S. boots on the ground may trigger a major international crisis."[59]

It was within the context of discussing the difficulties of counterterrorist action that the president addressed specifically the challenges involved in fighting against terrorists in Pakistan. He went on to suggest it was that difficult context that helped shape the choice to take "lethal, targeted action against al-Qaida and its associated forces, including with remotely piloted aircraft commonly referred to as drones." Obama admitted that the new technology has raised serious questions "about who is targeted, and why; about civilian casualties, and the risk of creating new enemies; about the legality of such strikes under U.S. and international law; about accountability and morality."[60] The president devoted a substantial part of the remainder of his remarks to addressing the questions he listed.

First, he asserted that the targeted drone strikes were effective, with documented evidence taken from al-Qaida leaders that indicated how the strikes had disrupted their operations. "Dozens of highly skilled al-Qaida commanders, trainers, bomb makers, and operatives have been taken off the battlefield. Plots have been disrupted that would have targeted international aviation, U.S. transit systems, European cities and our troops in Afghanistan. Simply put, these strikes have saved lives."[61]

Concerning the legality of the strikes, the president cited the AUMF as well as international law supporting a nation's right to defend itself from attack and to engage in armed conflict to defeat those who attacked first.

"We are at war with an organization that right now would kill as many Americans as they could if we did not stop them first. So this is a just war—a war waged proportionally, in last resort, and in self-defense."[62]

With regard to who is targeted, Obama was direct: "beyond the Afghan theater, we only target al-Qaida and its associated forces." Drones are not employed if the United States has the capability to capture a terrorist: "our preference is always to detain, interrogate, and prosecute." Drone strikes are not employed wherever the United States chooses: "our actions are bound by consultations with partners, and respect for state sovereignty."[63] Furthermore, targeted strikes are not taken "to punish individuals—we act against terrorists who pose a continuing and imminent threat to the American people, and when there are not other governments capable of effectively addressing the threat."[64]

The president also stated that the United States will not attack unless "there is near-certainty that no civilians will be killed or injured—the highest standard we can set." For Obama, that "point is critical" because he knew that much of the criticism directed against his administration's policy "centers on reports of civilian casualties." He acknowledged there was "a wide gap between U.S. assessments of such casualties and nongovernmental reports." The president recognized that despite serious efforts to limit civilian casualties the targeted drone strikes have caused unwanted deaths. He said such deaths "will haunt" him and others in the chain of command "for as long as we live." He went on, "but as Commander-in-Chief, I must weigh these heartbreaking tragedies against the alternatives. To do nothing in the face of terrorist networks would invite far more civilian casualties," not just in the United States but in the locales where terrorists have a foothold. He asked his listeners to remember that "the terrorists we are after target civilians, and the death toll from their acts of terrorism against Muslims dwarfs any estimate of civilian casualties from drone strikes."[65]

Obama then reflected upon the alternative to using targeted drone strikes in counterterrorism, namely, conventional military operations. Yet "even small Special Operations carry enormous risks. Conventional airpower or missiles are far less precise than drones, and likely to cause more civilian casualties and local outrage." And then there are the other negative aspects of using conventional forces because "invasions of these territories lead us to be viewed as occupying armies; unleash a torrent of unintended consequences; are difficult to contain; and ultimately empower those who thrive on violent conflict."[66]

While admitting that "the conflict with al-Qaida, like all armed conflict, invites tragedy," the president maintained that by using narrowly and precisely targeted acts against known terrorists the United States is following a policy that generates the least amount of civilian deaths. "[N]either conventional military action, nor waiting for attacks to occur, offers moral safe-harbor. Neither does a sole reliance on law enforcement in territories that have no functioning police or security services—and indeed, have no functioning law."[67]

Before leaving the topic of targeted drone strikes and moving onto other counterterrorism issues, the president spoke to the question of transparency, for the "very precision of drone strikes and the necessary secrecy often involved in such actions can end up shielding our government from the public scrutiny that a troop deployment invites."[68] Obama insisted that reports on every strike outside of the war zones of Afghanistan and Iraq have been delivered to the proper congressional committees. And that reporting includes the strike on Anwar al-Awlaki. The president announced he had authorized declassification of that strike as well as three other strikes where Americans were killed by attack drones. This was for the sake of transparency and to eliminate the more outrageous claims made about abusive executive power. The president also said that "when a U.S. citizen goes abroad to wage war against America and is actively plotting to kill U.S. citizens" then, if capture is not possible, "his citizenship should no more serve as a shield than a sniper shooting down on an innocent crowd should be protected from a SWAT team."[69]

During the address the president made a significant comment concerning policy guidance. "[O]ver the last four years, my administration has worked vigorously to establish a framework that governs our use of force against terrorists—insisting upon clear guidelines, oversight and accountability that is now codified in Presidential Policy Guidance that I signed yesterday."[70] Word of this document, often referred to as a "playbook," had entered into public knowledge in the fall of 2012. It was reported that one of the things that pushed the administration to develop the standards was the prospect that Obama would not win reelection and that Mitt Romney would assume the role of commander in chief. "There was a concern that the levers might no longer be in our hands," according to an anonymous administration official. Reportedly, "Mr. Obama did not want to leave an 'amorphous' program to his successor," the same official said.[71]

To be included in the playbook are "the process for adding names to kill lists, the legal principles that govern when U.S. citizens can be targeted overseas and the sequence of approvals required when the CIA or U.S. military conducts drone strikes outside war zones."[72] It was widely reported that John Brennan was a major actor in the development of the document. The fact that the playbook evolved over four years suggests that early on in the use of targeted drone strikes there was a lack of specific norms and processes that might guide U.S. actions. The newness of the weaponry had led to a situation where the nation's ability to engage in lethal actions outpaced our leaders' clarity of thought about the who, when, and where of decisions to employ drones in targeted killings.

On the same day as the speech by Obama, the White House released a brief document that had the appearance of being a nonclassified summary of the materials that might be found in the classified playbook.[73] The document is clear; "The policy of the United States is not to use lethal force when it is feasible to capture a terrorist suspect."[74] It then provides four "preconditions" that must be met before "lethal force will be used outside areas of active hostilities."

1. There must be a legal basis for using lethal force;
2. The target . . . poses a continuing imminent threat to U.S. persons. It is simply not the case that all terrorists pose [such a threat];
3. The following criteria must be met:

   a. Near certainty that the terrorist target is present;

b. Near certainty that noncombatants will not be injured or killed;
c. An assessment that capture is not feasible at the time of the operation;
d. An assessment that the relevant governmental authorities in the country where action is contemplated cannot or will not address the threat to U.S. persons;
e. An assessment that no other reasonable alternatives exist to effectively address the threat to U.S. persons.

4. International legal principles, including respect for sovereignty and the law of armed conflict, impose important constraints on the ability of the United States to act unilaterally.[75]

The document also states that the decision to use lethal force is made at the "most senior levels of the U.S. government, informed by departments and agencies with relevant expertise and institutional roles." These senior officials will make sure the standards are met and attorneys will "review and examine the legality of proposals." The analysis to determine whether a possible target "meets the legal and policy standards for the operation" will entail knowing the target's past and current activity in any plots, the value of the information the target possesses, the actual capability the target has to enact an attack, and the impact of U.S. operations on foreign relations. Further, if the target is a U.S. citizen "the Department of Justice will conduct an additional legal analysis" to determine if an attack is consistent with the Constitution and laws of the United States.[76]

Several points should be underscored. The president maintained in the speech his consistent claim that the United States is legally authorized to target the enemy wherever the enemy goes, although there is the limit of respect for the sovereignty of those states not part of the declared battlefields of Afghanistan and Iraq. However, these sovereign states also have duties as a result of their sovereignty over their territory, and that entails preventing terrorist activity within their borders when evidence is brought to their attention about such activity.

The summary statement's title also makes evident that the administration distinguishes between the standards for lethal strikes in the "hot battlefields" of Afghanistan and Iraq and the standards being set as policy for attacks beyond those declared war zones. It seems that by distinguishing between drone attacks within declared areas of armed conflict and strikes outside those areas, the president was looking ahead to the time when American combat troops would no longer be engaged in Afghanistan and Iraq. The standards he put forth, as a matter of policy and not law, explained the use of targeted drone strikes outside of battleground zones.[77]

The president still has the right to order the use of lethal force using drones or other means to defend the nation from imminent attack. That right is not founded upon the AUMF but international law and the U.S. Constitution. Key for asserting this right of defense is that the threat of attack is characterized as "imminent." In his speech the president used the word "continuing" along with "imminent." What is the significance of that terminology? Two commentators remarking on the speech suggest that pairing "continuing" with "imminent" "broadens the notion of imminence such that a threat is imminent in a continuous fashion."[78] A threat that is continuous is one that could occur at any point in time and so the imminence of the threat is ongoing. In other words, "given evidence of its nature, aims, and past behaviors" a group or organization is presumed to be always posing an imminent threat. This is a "non-temporal sense of the word 'imminent.'"[79] Such an interpretation is akin to Koh's "elongated imminence" or Brennan's claim in his Harvard speech that global terrorism has led many national leaders to see the need for a "more flexible understanding" of imminence.

Finally, the speech also clarified the president's understanding of feasibility. It does not mean something that is physically possible to do. Rather, feasible in the context of deciding whether to capture or use lethal force entails a judgment about risks to U.S. forces and also risks to civilians in the area where a capture operation is tried. Obama also talked about the political risks of putting American military personnel on the ground of another nation. So feasibility has to do with being able to capture a targeted individual without risking undue harm to tactical, strategic, and political interests.[80]

HOW DOES AN INDIVIDUAL BECOME A TARGET?

In an extensively researched essay, the international lawyer Gregory McNeal has assembled the best exposition of the actual practice of the Obama administration as it determines legitimate targets and decides whether to implement a targeted killing using a drone strike. The aim of McNeal's project was to discuss procedures for developing accountability in the targeted killing process. In this section my aim is narrower; I will present the findings of McNeal's study that describe how the policy works, that is, "how killing lists are made" and "how targeted killings are executed."[81]

Formulating lists of targets for attack in aerial bombardments is nothing new. There have been debates about the legitimacy of some targets in just about every modern war. What has focused the attention of commentators in the present context is the accuracy and precision of drone strikes. The accuracy of the weapons heightens the demand for intelligence about the proposed target to ensure that the correct person is attacked. Because a mistaken targeted killing leads to wrongful death, the target lists "are vetted through an elaborate bureaucratic process that allows for verification of intelligence information before a person is added to a kill list."[82]

The first step in adding a name to the list is circumscribed by the category of permissible targets according to the laws of war. So civilians are not permissible targets, "except those who are members of an organized armed group and those who are directly participating in hostilities." As was seen in the debate in Israel, the idea of direct participation in hostilities is time-conditioned, so it is the idea of membership in an armed group that would most likely get a person added to a kill list. However, as was also seen in the Israeli debate, the expression "member of an organized armed group" is also a controversial phrase. To illustrate, there was a time when it was unclear whether al-Shabaab in Somalia was an organized force sufficiently associated with al-Qaida so as to render it targetable. After the death of bin Laden, however, the leaders of al-Shabaab publicly vowed allegiance to al-Qaida.[83] So now al-Shabaab is considered an associated armed force.

Nonetheless, even supposing that a given group is organized, armed, and allied in a conflict, there remains the question of which members of the group may be targeted. Here there is a fundamental divide between the U.S. approach and the International Committee of the Red Cross (ICRC). The ICRC interprets the idea of "direct participation in hostilities" as pertaining to persons who fulfill a "continuous combat function," that is, are always engaged in "the preparation, execution, or command of acts or operations" in hostilities.[84] The United States, on the other hand, "claims the authority to target persons who are members of organized armed groups, based merely on their membership status."[85]

Following the determination of whether a person falls within the legal category of legitimate target there is a review of the initial judgment "to ensure that attacking an individual is lawful under the law of armed conflict or a particular covert action finding or executive directive."[86]

Moving beyond the legal analysis the process includes "analysis aimed at determining both the short- and long-term costs and benefits of striking a particular target." The "process is complex and time intensive, usually involving dozens of analysts from different agencies." The sole aim is "to ensure that any person whose name appears on a kill list has been identified, vetted, and validated." Only after this study is complete may a person then "be nominated for placement on a kill list" and approval of any nomination lies "at the highest levels of government," which often means the explicit approval of the president.[87]

Even if membership in al-Qaida or its associated forces is sufficient to be considered a legitimate target, it is important to note, as both Obama and Brennan did in their public speeches, that a specific decision to place a name on a target list is done on the basis of "effects-based targeting." The decision requires examination of what the impact of a target's death would be on the terrorist organization.[88] Similar to Koh's criterion of uniqueness versus fungibility, the analysis must show that the targeted killing will have substantive negative effects upon the group rather than killing a person who is easily replaced.

Still the targeting process does not focus solely on leaders. There may be lower-level actors whose skill sets or resources make them valuable to a terrorist organization. It has been reported by at least one source, Reuters, that the CIA has killed far more low-level than high-level al-Qaida personnel since the drone strikes began in 2008.[89] This may be due to the lesson learned from the Israeli campaign, that "the effects sought by killing are not merely the immediate effects of eliminating a person, but also the second- and third-order effects such as pressuring, desynchronizing, and debilitating the effectiveness of terrorist networks."[90]

When national security analysts ponder the grave question, who is worth killing, they start out with the premise that al-Qaida and its associated forces are social networks, not hierarchical, centralized organizations. This outlook encourages a study of a terrorist group as a system of "nodes connected by links and assesses how components" of the group "operate together and independently of one another." The hope is to apply "pressure to various nodes and links within networks to disrupt and degrade their functionality."[91]

Developing a "pattern of life analysis" whereby analysts trace the relationships between people and places takes time. Both human and electronic surveillance "tracks and notes every person visited. Connections between the target, the sites they visit, and the persons they interact with are documented, built into a network diagram," and analyzed. Gradually a pattern emerges of the political, economic, and social networks that support the terrorist group. Everything from money trails to family histories is traced. And this explains why apparent low-level personnel such as couriers can be critical players in a network. Abu Ahmed al-Kuwaiti was bin Laden's only means of communication with the rest of al-Qaida.[92]

So it is not titles or ranks the analysts study; they seek to discern what is called "criticality." It is this that is the most important element in deciding whether a nominated target goes on a kill list. Four factors are included in analyzing how critical a possible target is to the group: (1)

importance in the group's ability to conduct operations; (2) the time between the death of the target and its impact upon the group; (3) the time needed for the group to recover from the killing and regain its functional capability; and (4) an assessment of the degree to which a death will affect the group's current output compared to its maximum output.

For example, if the nominated target is a bomb maker, the analysis would assess how valuable the specific bomb maker is to the terror group, using the four factors listed above. How will a targeted killing of the bomb maker impact the group's ability to conduct terrorist operations? If the group has multiple persons skilled at bomb making then the group might not suffer significant short-term consequences from the targeted killing and be able to recover swiftly and restore its full operations. Long-term, however, it may be that training a new bomb maker takes a good deal of time and effort. Or it may be hard to recruit bomb makers if it is known that they are a targeted group. These are the considerations that go into a criticality assessment.[93]

Besides the element of criticality the other key element in determining who to approve for a kill list is the "susceptibility" of a target to attack. The concern is for the location of the target, mobility, and countermeasures available to the target. Over time intelligence may be gathered that indicates when a target is most vulnerable to attack. "[I]t is rare that a lack of vulnerability will prevent a target from making it to a nomination list for consideration; rather it is more likely to affect the prioritization of the target, require additional assets to monitor the target, alter how the target may be attacked, and may even determine what government agency is responsible" to implement the attack.[94]

All the analysis generates an extensive paper trail, electronic and hard copy. A folder for each potential target is created with notations of gaps in the needed intelligence, requests for legal opinions, and notes for briefing materials. These "target folders are continuously updated to reflect the most recent information regarding a target's status, the compiled data is independently reviewed by personnel not responsible for its collection."[95] And it is reported that names may be taken off a kill list if the information becomes outdated.[96]

As the material needed for vetting a potential nominee is compiled there is an ongoing process of assessment done by various agencies and at interagency meetings. Once this is done "a validation step follows the vetting step," the purpose of which is "to ensure that all proposed targets meet the objectives and criteria outlined in strategic guidance" as well as comply with domestic law and the laws of armed conflict and rules of engagement.[97] McNeal maintains that "many of the concerns that critics say should be weighed in the targeted killing process are considered prior to nominating a target for inclusion on a kill list."[98]

Once the vetting and validation processes are completed, the case for a nominee is debated by officials higher in the government. The materials in the target's file are condensed and worked up as a set of PowerPoint slides, known colloquially as "baseball cards." Beginning in the Bush administration and continuing during the Obama years, it is the "expectation that senior bureaucrats will vote on whether names should be formally approved for killing."[99] The vote need not be unanimous, but a vote to abstain, oppose, or concur with comment will indicate "greater operational and strategic risk" that the president or other final approval authority will note when making a decision. It is reported that a substantial number of the final approvals are done by Obama personally.[100]

HOW IS A TARGETED KILLING IMPLEMENTED?

Once a name is approved for addition to the target list, how do U.S. personnel go about the task of attacking a target? An extensive process has developed to make sure the target is the person on the kill list. There is also "an elaborate process" for "mitigating the incidental harm to nearby civilians and civilian objects."[101] The United States insists that all targeted killings are conducted according to the law of armed conflict. The steps taken for executing a targeted killing have been summarized as finding, fixing, tracking, and targeting.

Finding involves identifying and locating the target. In order to do that, multiple intelligence sources are employed. Electronic signals intelligence may locate a target but be unable to determine who it is. Airborne sensors with video will track a target, but not be able to identify the person. Human intelligence can learn intent but be incapable of pinpointing a precise location. Taken together, however, these sources will normally be adequate to find a target even amid a crowd.[102]

Once a target is found, the fixing step involves the determination of the "probable future location of the target, as well as positive identification" that the individual is the person on the kill list. Fixing a target means reconnaissance and surveillance that draw upon the "pattern-of-life-analysis" used to learn the individual's movements and relationships. The target is tracked and monitored so that "at some point in time, the attacker is able to determine a specific location at which the target will be located."[103] Then the attacker would have the decision to fire upon the target or not. The presumption is that a potential target is a civilian until proven otherwise. So positive identification is a threshold that must be met.[104]

The major reason an actual attack does not occur is the concern for harm to civilians or the civilian environment, for example, dams, religious shrines, or power grids. Knowing the "effects range" of the weapon to be used, the "military commander and his subordinates place a point on a map representing the target, draw an effects radius around that target, and assess what known collateral concerns exist within that radius."[105] It is not uncommon for the commander to have a target monitored for many hours until the individual is no longer near civilians or civilian objects. During this entire period there must be an "unbroken chain of custody—from first identification all the way to attack." If the target is lost sight of by walking into a building or under a grove of trees the entire identification process begins anew or the targeted killing operation is canceled.[106]

If there is an assessment of risk to noncombatants, the commanders have various measures that can be taken to mitigate the harmful effects of an attack, either by using more accurate or less powerful weapons, or by "weaponeering," which are measures to lessen the effects of the weapon by utilizing different approaches based on factors like wind direction or topography. Should such measures still result in an assessment that indicates likely harm to civilians or civilian objects then a proportionality analysis is undertaken.[107]

A judgment of proportionality is never a precise calculation. According to the laws of war, proportionality in the *jus in bello* is a determination that the loss of civilian life or injury to civilians resulting from a military action is excessive when compared to the direct military advantage to be gained. There is no predetermined number of dead or injured that makes an attack "excessive." The judgment is on a case-by-case basis, as the harm caused in attacking a key al-Qaida leader may be deemed tolerable, but the same harm would be excessive if the attack was against a less significant target. There are established guidelines as to who is the authority to make that judgment. Depending upon a wide array of variables, such as the theater of operations, the agency involved, or the strategic goal, the approving authority could be a general officer, the CIA director, the secretary of defense, or the president.[108]

SUMMING UP

Recognizing that the Obama administration's policy has evolved and likely continues to evolve, there is reasonable certainty that the present policy on targeted killing and the use of drones looks something like the following. The National Counterterrorism Center is the central body that coordinates and oversees the interagency process of vetting persons proposed for targeting. Personnel, military and intelligence, from a variety of agencies, compile data and nominate individuals. The National Counterterrorism Center then takes over the process for further vetting and reviews the proposed targets to see if they meet the standards of the White House for a targeted killing. If so, the presidential counterterrorism advisor convenes a meeting of the National Security Council deputies to receive the input of senior officials from the CIA, FBI, and Defense and State Departments, as well as the National Counterterrorism Center. It is at this stage that lawyers from Defense and State would offer legal opinions and if there are objections the process is usually stalled until questions are resolved.

If there is approval at the level of the National Security Council meeting, then the president's counterterrorism advisor puts together a presentation for the president's final approval. This final presentation ensures that the information about the target is complete and accurate, the targeted killing will serve the objectives of the counterterrorism campaign, the rationale for the targeted killing is detailed and persuasive, and the nature and probability of collateral damage are presented.

Of course, as Attorney General Eric Holder explained in his Northwestern speech, any use of lethal force by the United States should comply with the four fundamental principles—necessity, distinction, proportionality, and humanity—of international humanitarian law that governs the use of force.

In light of the care and thoroughness that the Obama administration gives to the formulation of target lists and the painstaking planning that goes into an actual targeted killing operation, it may seem surprising that there are so many critics of the U.S. policy. Yet the criticism is abundant. In the final chapter we will look at the most serious criticisms and suggest areas where the policy and practice of drones in targeted killing ought to change.

5

THE FUTURE CONTEXT

Addressing the Moral Issues

The present counterterrorism policy of the United States permits the use of drone strikes in targeted killings. Neither the use of drones nor the idea of targeted killings is without controversy. There is no lack of critics who have provided thoughtful challenges to the U.S. policy. Nor is there a lack of supporters defending the policy. This chapter will review major objections to the policy and weigh their merit. In other words, the aim of this final chapter is to move beyond descriptive language to undertake a normative assessment of U.S. drone policy. The ethical analysis inevitably entails using words like "should" and "ought" to provide moral guidance for future policy. My comments will be organized under eight distinct but related areas that present the most salient challenges to the way the United States employs drones in a program of targeted killing. The crucial objective at hand is to determine whether U.S. policy or elements of that policy are wise and morally justifiable.

We might begin, however, with a brief acknowledgment of what many see as the benefits of using drones for targeted killing. These have been summarized by Michael Boyle, a scholar of international relations, in the following way: (1) drones have been effective in killing terrorists while minimizing civilian casualties; (2) drones are successful in killing HVTs in terrorist organizations; (3) targeted killing with drones puts significant pressure on terrorist groups by degrading their ability to plot, plan, and undertake attacks; and (4) when compared to other means of counterterrorism the use of drones has a clear cost-benefit advantage.[1] These benefits have led at least one author to claim that the use of drone strikes is not only militarily effective, but also morally obligatory due to the number of civilian lives saved by such discriminating weapons, as well as the lives of U.S. and allied combat personnel spared in attacks from terrorists killed by drone raids.[2] In our moral assessment of drone use we ought to consider these claims for if they are true they make a good case on behalf of the U.S. drone policy.

As we have seen, criticism of present U.S. policy regarding the use of drones in targeted killing comes in a variety of guises. Are we targeting the wrong people? Do we kill large numbers of civilians accidentally? Are there alternatives to the use of drones? Will the present policy lead to attainment of the long-range goals of American foreign policy? What if other nations adopt our approach in their use of drones? These and other questions will be taken up in the pages that follow.

DISCRIMINATION

By its very definition an act of targeted killing ought to be highly discriminatory. The fact that drone attacks often occur not on battlegrounds in counterinsurgency conflict but in counterterrorist operations beyond declared combat zones suggests that there should be special care taken that no innocent persons will be harmed. While "collateral damage" in war may be justified if genuine efforts at using discriminate and proportionate means were made, Americans are not tolerant of police actions that cost civilian lives in our society. When the theater of operations is not an established combat area there must be reasonable certainty that no innocents will be killed. That is what President Obama declared as U.S. policy in May 2013, stating that there must be "near certainty that no civilians would be killed or injured."[3] However, in that same speech the president acknowledged that there are many concerns about whom the United States targets and how that is determined. For that reason the issue of discrimination remains controversial in the counterterrorism policy of the United States.

A common charge against the use of targeted killings is that they are employed against individuals who are not legitimate targets or, at least, that the legitimacy of the target has not been adequately ascertained. There is no norm of the just war tradition more fundamental than that which directs combatants to avoid the deliberate killing of noncombatants.[4] How might one determine whether the victim of a targeted killing policy is a morally legitimate target? This is a hotly debated topic when assessing U.S. policy.

A question behind the question about targeting is the issue of whether the appropriate paradigm for the present counterterrorism strategy is that of warfare or law enforcement. Ethical standards change for determining the legitimacy of targeting an individual depending upon whether the target is deemed a combatant (legal or illegal) in war, or a civilian engaged in illegal activity and best understood as a criminal.

Although the practice of targeted killing raises a number of ethical dilemmas, there is none bigger than determining the justification for targeting a specific individual. Targeted killing underscores the difficulty of categorizing the actors and actions involved in contemporary armed conflicts against agents of terrorism. I share the view of Michael Gross that employing targeted killing in the struggle against terrorism "complicates the conceptual framework that justifies killing during war and distinguishes it from murder."[5]

As noted in chapter 3, the debate over targeted killing was largely occasioned by the adoption of a targeted killing policy by Israel in response to the second Intifada. A major aspect of that debate was determining whether the "conceptual framework" for assessing the targeted killing policy should be that of police action or military action. Should terrorists be thought of as criminals or combatants? As was recounted in chapter 3, there was a notable shift in Israeli thinking toward a military framework.

The development in Israeli thinking was due, first of all, to the inapplicability of the law enforcement model owing to the fact that the terrorists were not under the jurisdiction of the Israeli state. And there was also strong reason to doubt the Palestinian Authority was capable and willing to move against the terrorists. Furthermore, if a violent criminal resists arrest, the police may use lethal force to end the threat of escape. Analogously, one might suggest that a terrorist operating outside of the usual restraints of state jurisdiction (or within a state complicit with terrorist activity) is to be regarded as choosing that locale in order to resist arrest and is thereby subject to lethal force.[6]

Second, there was the fact that the terror attacks were not sporadic and isolated but systematic and regular, with a clear organizational network behind them. The scale of the violence had risen to the level of an armed conflict even if one party was not a state.

Third, the terrorists themselves rejected the idea that they were civilian criminals. They may not have used terms like "freedom fighter" or "guerrilla warrior," but they understood themselves to be combatants in an armed conflict. Following the decision of the Israeli High Court that the situation was one of "armed conflict of an international character," its authority effectively established the prevailing view that the nature of the fight against terror was more akin to the armed conflict model than the law enforcement model.

Yet the international law of war did not adequately address the reality of international terror organizations since the law presumed armed conflict to be between nations or between combatants within a nation such as a war of secession. The case of international terror organizations beyond the borders of the victim state engaging in sustained violent attacks did not fit the standards presumed by the law.

The unusual feature of terrorists was that they do not follow the norms of international humanitarian law in their combat. As many commentators have pointed out, terrorists do not obey the criteria for combatant status that are set out in the Geneva Conventions. Nor do they observe the crucial distinction between civilian and combatant targets. For the terrorist, the death of noncombatants is not unwanted "collateral damage," for civilian deaths are the intended aim of a terrorist attack. Thus, terrorists may be combatants, but they are illegal combatants. And that status does not change merely because they pose as civilians for a brief time while being able to quickly revert back to their combatant roles. Furthermore, the terrorist's action is not reducible to the actual incident of the attack. The terror activity includes as well the plotting of tactics, the acquisition of weapons, the training of personnel, and other significant elements necessary for the launching of an attack.

Still, if the counterterrorist strategy is to be ethically informed there must be a legitimate cause for engaging in a targeted killing. Here the Israeli debate underscored an important point. The purpose of targeted killing as part of a strategy of counterterrorism must be defense of the innocent through interdiction of terrorist activity. Targeted killing ought not be used as punishment or retribution for past misdeeds. That would lead targeted killing into the realm of extrajudicial execution. The use of targeted killing ought to be restricted to stopping the commission of a terrorist attack upon innocent persons. We shall discuss an important aspect of this conclusion later in this chapter under the subheading "Imminence." But first, we ought to consider a practice that fails the ethical test of discrimination when choosing a target.

Signature Strikes

Perhaps the most controversial case of targeted killing is that of signature strikes, when people are targeted not because they are specifically identified as being on an extensively vetted and officially approved kill list,[7] but on the grounds that they exhibit behavior that renders them suspect. Signature strikes refer to attacks premised on a person demonstrating a set of "signature" behaviors that the United States connects with militant activity. This is differentiated from "personality" strikes, which are true targeted killings in that the identity of the target is known.[8] In counterinsurgency operations on a declared battleground, there is no requirement that the identity of a targeted individual be known. In areas outside of active hostilities, however, to engage in lethal attacks on the basis of a "pattern of life" analysis is unacceptable, I believe, given the presumption of innocence that must be accorded to the life of anyone not positively identified as a threat to others' lives. Critics of the policy insist its rationale is inadequate and that evidence of direct participation in violent hostilities is needed before attacking someone.[9]

In early 2008, then President George Bush approved the practice of attacking vehicle convoys even without positive identification of the occupants, as long as they appeared to be al-Qaida or Taliban leaders and there was low risk of casualties apart from the convoy participants. By the summer of that year the standard had become even more permissive, a "sort of 'reasonable man' standard. If it seemed reasonable, you could hit it."[10]

At the outset of his presidency, Barack Obama expressed disagreement with the practice. Obama wanted confirmation of the identities of the targets before signing off on an attack. However, there are reports Obama has permitted the practice of signature strikes to continue in Pakistan as well as in Yemen, even though the criteria for an attack are stricter than what he inherited from his predecessor.[11] Due to the lack of transparency on the part of both the Bush and Obama administrations regarding their policies, there are not a lot of known specifics about signature strikes.

In an environment where the United States has angered and injured many civilians, the mere fact that a person supports a terrorist group is not evidence that the individual is actively playing a planning or operational role in terrorist activity. The laws of war distinguish between civilians working as drivers, medics, or cooks in support roles from those who are combatants. While the job descriptions may be fuzzier in terrorist networks, it is still possible that an individual who has lost a family member due to prior American action may be sympathetic enough to a terrorist organization to play a fringe role of support by rushing to the scene of a drone strike to assist victims. To be targeted in a "double-tap," or follow-up strike, solely for that reason is morally dubious.[12] Responding to the victims of an attack is a natural human reaction; it should not be the basis on which one's own life is lost. A major source for information about casualties in Pakistan has claimed that more than fifty civilians have died in follow-up attacks against those coming to the relief of victims of a first strike. As a result, families and emergency workers are reluctant to come to the aid of those injured in drone attacks. One humanitarian agency established a policy forbidding workers to approach a stricken area less than six hours after an attack.[13]

Further, to be targeted because one is an armed male while living in an environment where people carry weapons on a routine basis is an unduly expansive view of legitimate targeting. The policy of designating all military-age males as presumed combatants goes against the usual presumption of just war reasoning that a person is a noncombatant unless there is clear evidence to the contrary. In actuality, signature strikes are not true examples of targeted killing because they are hardly targeted at a known individual. The key advantage of a targeted killing is its alleged precision, but that advantage is taken away if targets are chosen without sufficient identification.

The United States is not doing targeted killing when it attacks meetings, village assemblies, and in December 2012 when it attacked a wedding party in Yemen. Twelve men were killed as they accompanied the bride and her family to the neighboring town of the groom. Although the U.S. government maintains all the men were militants, the Yemeni government disagrees, calling the strike a tragic mistake that killed only civilians. One thing that is known is that an unidentified donor paid out more than $800,000 in cash as compensation to the families of the victims. The Yemeni government does not provide that kind of compensation to its citizens. If it was an American agent, that is not something the United States does when it is convinced it has killed the right people.[14] If one knows a group is composed of terrorist militants, then it is possible to target those people, but in the case of signature strikes, the United States does not know; rather, it assumes the group's identity and that is inappropriate as a basis for lethal action.

A study in 2014 by the Stimson Center's Task Force on Drone Policy posed the issue this way. Imagine living in the Federally Administered Tribal Areas of Pakistan or a rural village in Yemen. From the perspective of people who live in those regions affected by drone strikes, "there is no way for an individual to be certain whether he is considered targetable by the United States." The report poses several questions:

> Would attending a meeting or community gathering also attended by an al-Qaida member make him targetable? Would renting a building or selling a vehicle to a member of an "associated" force render him targetable? What counts as an "associated force?" Would accepting financial or medical aid from a terrorist group make him a target? Would extending hospitality to a relative who is affiliated with a terrorist group lead the Unites States to consider him a target?[15]

Caught in such uncertainty, normal life becomes impossible, and should an attack come from the United States it will appear arbitrary. Furthermore, the people living in these regions of the world lack the ability to seek clarification of their status or appeal it to an impartial and effective arbitrator.

Recall that the Obama administration's stated targeting policy has three thresholds: the individual is a member of al-Qaida or an associated force, the target is an imminent threat, and there is near certainty of no civilian casualties. The practice of signature strikes fails to pass those declared policy thresholds.

An additional factor to consider is that the original aim of the targeted killing program was to hunt down HVTs in al-Qaida and its associated networks. Signature strikes, even when successful in attacking militants, almost always have been directed at minor or low-level figures in terrorist groups. One report posits "the number of high-level targets killed as a percentage of total casualties is extremely low—estimated at just 2%."[16]

In a nutshell, signature strikes are morally problematic since there is too little assurance that the targets are legitimate. Too many assumptions are made with too little firm evidence that the targets constitute a clear or imminent danger. Thus, it is doubtful that the practice of signature strikes passes the ethical test of discrimination in targeting.

IMMINENCE

Beyond signature strikes, another point of criticism of U.S. targeting policy has been the way the word "imminent" is used in the assertion that individuals are targeted because they constitute an imminent threat to the United States.[17] The Obama administration invokes self-defense as a justification for using drone strikes. That is, of course, a strong argument if it can be shown to be true. However, the requirement of the just war tradition, as well as international humanitarian law, is that any preemptive attack undertaken as an act of self-defense may only be launched in the face of an *imminent* threat.

Oddly, in the view of many, the Justice Department determined that imminence no longer means that an attack will "take place in the immediate future." While that may surprise those who consult dictionaries, imminence is now to be understood so that it effectively means not that al-Qaida is about to attack the United States, but that the United States has a promising window of opportunity to launch an attack against al-Qaida. Using language in this way has an Alice in Wonderland feel to it.[18]

Defenders of the revisionist rendering of imminence, however, claim there is good reason for the change due to the reality that al-Qaida is always in the midst of plotting terrorist attacks, even if not enacting them. Therefore, al-Qaida and its associated forces constitute an ongoing threat, and since we cannot know what a terrorist organization is up to at any given time, the assumption must be that any member of al-Qaida or associated forces is an imminent threat.[19] As Amitai Etzioni has argued, al-Qaida and other terrorist groups "are not dual-purpose organizations; one does not join them to provide social services and maybe engage in terrorism."[20] To be a member of al-Qaida is sufficient to qualify as a candidate for targeting in a manner analogous to considering an enemy soldier a legitimate target even if the individual is not actually attacking at the time.[21]

Yet Kenneth Roth worries that treating every supposed leader or low-level member of al-Qaida as an imminent threat is too broad. After all, police have the power to use deadly force before an imminent threat, but not the right to summarily execute every alleged wrongdoer.[22] The question must be asked, is there really *no* need to demonstrate *any* evidence of direct participation in threatening activity before killing someone?

The difficulty in the present case is that terrorists do not indicate their intent the way that conventional armies commonly do. The terrorist threat falls into an ambiguous area where the threat is more than a gathering one, but not necessarily imminent. A different standard is needed. So defenders of targeted killing, like Etzioni, propose membership in al-Qaida or its associated forces as the trip wire for action since those groups have a clear intent to kill others. Yet it may be that the proposal is too broad for the reasons noted above when discussing signature strikes. The stated intent of U.S. policy is that targeted killings are used to eliminate HVTs in the struggle against terrorism and that is closer to the ethical mark than Etzioni's willingness to include blanket membership in the group.

At the same time it must be said that it strains common sense to suggest that a person is no longer a combatant simply because he or she has left the battlefield or is not carrying a weapon. There is a well-known topic in the ethics of combat that might be called the "naked soldier," which has been used to illustrate the distinction between combatants and civilians. The case involves a military sniper who comes within range of an enemy soldier bathing in a river. It is clear from the uniform and weapon lying on the shore that the individual is an enemy combatant. May the sniper shoot to kill the naked soldier? Michael Walzer has argued that not only *may* the sniper shoot the naked soldier, but there is a duty for the sniper to do so.[23]

Walzer acknowledges that some will find this emotionally reprehensible. It may be true that the enemy soldier, once he finishes his washing, will put on his uniform, pick up his gun, and become a dangerous threat to other soldiers on the same side as the sniper. Yet, in the moment, the naked soldier reveals the vulnerability and humanity that all combatants share. To shoot at that moment requires a cold-bloodedness that will strike many as wrong.

Yet consider another case, one that is more common in the experience of war. Behind the battle lines a group of soldiers are resting from the heat of battle. They may be napping, eating, playing cards, or showering. A large artillery shell is fired or an aerial attack drops a bomb that lands in the camp and kills many of these resting soldiers. Such deaths, tragic as they may be, do not violate the norms of war. Soldiers are part of a class of people who put themselves at risk by being people who threaten others. That they are not a threat at the moment they are eating or sleeping does not remove them from the class of people who are warriors, and they are legitimate targets. For in a matter of minutes they may once again be on the front lines and active agents in a combat situation.

Now if those soldiers were eating or sleeping in a hospital or a POW camp there would be moral outrage if they were intentionally targeted. Enemy soldiers who are no longer threats, due to hospitalization or surrender, are not legitimate targets. They have, for the duration of their capture or medical care, ceased to be a threat. This is so even though POWs have a duty to escape when that is possible. So it is not about intentionality or some change of heart. It is a matter of no longer being a credible threat and therefore no longer a legitimate target for lethal action.

While the naked soldier may evoke a compassionate reaction when viewed from the crosshairs of a telescopic lens, it can be asked if he is most similar to the soldiers behind the front lines or those soldiers who are hospitalized or captured. By virtue of his readiness and ability to be transformed into a lethal threat to others, the naked soldier is akin to the soldiers resting before returning to the front lines. He remains an ongoing threat and a legitimate target. And this has long been accepted even in those cases where the enemy combatant is likely to have been a conscript and not a volunteer. How much more so is the terrorist a legitimate target when we consider that in all likelihood he or she has volunteered to participate in terrorist activity?

Returning to the situation of the terrorists, there is the question of whether they are to be treated as civilians with immunity to direct attack or combatants with the risk of being intentionally targeted. The challenge is to determine an individual's status absent the traditional markings of uniforms, insignia, and weapons. The person without these is a civilian. But civilians who take an active role in armed conflict are illegal combatants. In effect, they are civilians who surrender the right to be treated as a civilian for as long as they participate in terrorist acts. As the Israeli High Court suggested, civilians who take a direct role in a terrorist act do not have the same right of immunity from attack as civilians who are not direct participants in combat.

Also to be considered is the declared intent of the terrorist. Terrorists from al-Qaida or its associated forces commonly announce that they are at war with the United States, avowing their intent to attack and kill Americans. It does not seem convincing for terrorists to claim the right to kill as a combatant in war while also claiming the same protection as (criminal) civilians deserving of legal due process.[24]

It cannot be that a participant in an armed conflict is granted a status change by simple gestures that can be quickly and easily reversed once there is no risk involved. That is the lesson of the naked soldier. The Israeli political scientist Michael Gross has suggested that a careful process of compiling a kill list of known active terrorists can be understood as an attempt at establishing whether a person should be treated as a combatant or a civilian. If identified as an active terrorist, then he or she is vulnerable in the same way that a uniformed combatant is a legitimate target of attack. That judgment suggests two conclusions. First, such an approach would continue to rule out signature strikes, for the target must be a *known* terrorist. Second, the approach calls for a more careful delineation of who counts as an "active terrorist" than Etzioni's proposal of mere membership in an organization.

If mere membership is too broad a standard for determining whether a person may be subject to a targeted killing, what standard should be utilized? Here the Israeli debate is helpful once again. Individuals deemed legitimate targets ought to be restricted to those who are active participants in a terrorist action. What constitutes active participation is a much-debated point. Recall that the Israeli High Court offered examples of what should count as taking part in actual hostility or conflict: the collection of intelligence about the other side; providing transportation of illegal combatants to or from hostilities; servicing, operating, or supervising the weapons of illegal combatants. While these illustrations do not provide a neat definition, they do suggest that the class of persons who are targetable is wider than those terrorists caught in the midst of specific lethal actions. Clearly there is a causal chain involved in terrorist activity and the use of targeted killing to interdict an attack may occur at various points along the chain.

The ICRC has produced a document to provide its understanding of the claim that someone is a participant in armed hostilities under the laws of war.[25] The hope was that the ICRC text would clarify the meaning of a "functional combatant" in armed conflict. However, the ICRC position has been subject to criticism since it was presented in 2009, including complaints by several of those who were involved in the extensive consultation conducted in the formulation of the document. Nonetheless, as the international lawyer Robert Chesney has stated, "the basic outlines of DPH [direct participation in hostilities] are clear enough and adequately identified in the *Interpretive Guidance*."[26] Chesney summarizes the meaning of DPH as (1) an activity likely to cause harm, (2) entailing direct causation of the harm rather than indirect, and (3) done to support one party in the conflict.[27]

A terrorist posing an immediate threat certainly counts as directly participating in hostilities, but who else? Possibly an individual providing vital support to persons posing an immediate danger; person(s) dispatching others to pose an immediate danger; persons preparing devices or supplying elements of devices to be used in terrorist acts; persons planning an act of terror; persons recruiting others to carry out terrorist acts; persons making operational decisions related to terrorist activities.[28] These are all causal agents playing vital roles in bringing about a terrorist action and who can, to use the language of the classic principle of cooperation, plausibly be described as engaged in formal and proximate material cooperation.[29]

Drone strikes are widely accepted if they stop terrorists caught in the midst of terrorist activity. In such a case it is clearly an act of self-defense or assistance in the defense of another innocent person. The problem is that drone strikes occur in additional contexts beyond the actual act of terrorism. Can such strikes be justified on the basis of legitimate anticipatory self-defense or preemption in the face of an imminent threat?

John Brennan in his April 2012 address made clear that targeted killing is not about vengeance for past crimes but an individual is targeted when it is "necessary to mitigate an actual ongoing threat—to stop plots, prevent future attacks, and save American lives."[30] The use of a drone strike is defensive in the sense that the targeted individual is known to be a person engaged in terrorist activity.

Brennan was insistent that launching a strike due to the ongoing threat of a terror attack did not equate with mere anxiety that a terrorist might attack someday. Rather the individual targeted would be an operational leader for al-Qaida or associated forces, an actual operative in the midst of training for or planning a plot, or a person with a unique skill set that is "being leveraged in a planned attack."[31]

Recall that in his most extensive comments on the matter, President Obama paired the words "continuing" and "imminent" so that imminence changed from a temporal term to something along the lines of Harold Koh's "elongated imminence." That is, the threat could occur at any time because the past evidence about the group's nature and aims demonstrates it is always posing a threat.

Changing the ordinary, commonsense temporal meaning of imminence to something else is fraught with risk for the protection of human life. We ought not allow targeted killing simply based on the chance that somewhere al-Qaida is plotting an attack and some individual who is a member of that group may in the future have a role in that attack. We need a stricter view of imminence than that in determining if a person poses a genuine threat that justifies targeted killing.

At the same time, as Tom Malinowski, formerly of Human Rights Watch, has put it, "I don't think that the 'imminence' rule would require the U.S. to show that an al-Qaida planner was literally on his way to the airport to put a bomb on a plane to Chicago before launching a strike. But it would require an individualized determination that the target is actively involved in planning future attacks (as against simply having been involved in terrorism in the past)."[32]

This approach seems to strike a balance between those who would insist that the United States could not launch a drone strike without "plot-specific knowledge"[33] of a terrorist's action and those who would permit such a strike if a person is simply a member of a group that is involved with terrorism. What can be sensibly demanded is that the government have "substantial evidence to support the belief that the person in question will in fact be involved in further attacks,"[34] and involved in a manner that constitutes direct and active participation as discussed earlier.

Before ending this subsection it should be stressed that determining whether an individual is a legitimate target is only one consideration in targeted killing, albeit a crucial one. Again, as both the distant and proximate contexts for the contemporary debate demonstrated, there is a long moral tradition on the use of lethal force and the presence of a just cause is but one criterion to employ in justifying deadly force. The issues of last resort or necessity, utility or reasonable hope of success, and proportionality or minimalizing collateral damage are all vital concerns in formulating a targeted killing policy. These other moral criteria must now be addressed. Targeted killing may have a narrow range of use in counterterrorism, provided a target's direct and active participation is evident in activity that is a threat to others and if the moral criteria stemming from the just war tradition are taken into proper account.

DEATH AND HARM TO CIVILIANS

What about the toll on civilians of our use of armed drones? This question is critical. Harm to civilians is, of course, key in any ethical examination of war. Tragically, we have witnessed a huge increase in the proportion of civilian deaths to combatant deaths in modern warfare.[35] In the majority of armed conflicts in modern times there have been vastly more civilians killed than soldiers.[36] If the use of drones were to continue to increase the ratio of civilian to combatant deaths it would be a telling criticism of drones.

The question of drone casualties, however, is controversial. There is no official report on casualties provided by any government source, U.S.

or otherwise. Indeed, there is no agreed upon figure for the total number of persons killed, even less the status of the victims as combatant or civilian. Estimates vary widely as to how many of the dead caused by drone attacks are civilians. As one harsh critic of drones acknowledges, the "estimates of the ratio of civilians to militants killed are all over the map."[37] This is because the major sources for information on casualties rely on local news stories and then use various approaches to interpreting the data.

For example, the terminology used by the three main sources of casualty data varies from "civilian" to "possible civilian" to "militant" to "alleged militant" to "unknown." The Bureau of Investigative Journalism (BIJ), based in London, mainly uses the term "alleged militant" to describe those killed who are presumed to be affiliated with terrorist groups, while the New America Foundation (NAF) and Long War Journal (LWJ), both in Washington, DC, simply use "militant." The NAF uses the militant designation to describe all organized, named groups bearing arms that are not recognized as officially Pakistani, Somali, or Yemeni military, police, or militia. If two or more local sources call someone a "militant" then so does the NAF and they follow that two-source method to identify civilians as well. If only one source calls the victims "civilians" the NAF lists them as "unknown." The LWJ does not explain how it classifies casualties.[38]

One source "defines all drone deaths as civilians unless the report clearly specifies which terrorist organization the dead belonged to." This leads to an estimate that 88 percent of deaths from drone strikes are civilian. Another source also relies on news reports but estimates "the civilian fatality rate to be only 32 percent relative to 68 percent militants." This source tabulates "any individuals whose status is unknown as 'militants' rather than civilians." And a third source for casualty reports gives a lower percentage of civilian deaths that is arrived at "by excluding all men and teenage boys from the 'civilian' category."[39]

Since all the sources rely upon local news, the casualty figures are based on reported, not actual, deaths. Journalists are not always adept at distinguishing civilians from combatants, and some reports combine known militants with alleged militants determined by age and gender. Broadening the category of who counts as a militant leads to a high likelihood of underreporting civilian casualties. Other local news reports do not provide firm figures, using vague words like "some" or "many" that then get translated differently into specific numbers by the various sources.[40]

Finally, many reports do not distinguish between drone attacks in declared battle zones when the drone was used in conventional counterinsurgency violence and drone attacks as part of a counterterrorism policy of targeted killing. The proportion of casualties, civilian and combatant, might vary greatly if the two different uses of attack drones were distinguished. The Afghan war has been fought as a counterinsurgency operation from the earliest days of the Obama administration. An important component of counterinsurgency theory is to win the support of the local population. This may have led to a calculation of proportionality that placed greater restraint upon drone attacks that risked local support for the counterinsurgency. The CIA operations in Pakistan have not followed the same strategy.

When civilians are killed by drone strikes in declared combat areas it is usually due to one of two circumstances: the unobserved nearness of civilians to the locale of an airstrike, or ground troops calling for a strike when mistakenly thinking civilians were enemy combatants. The U.S. military has acknowledged accidental civilian deaths on multiple occasions. The military's use of drones is a matter of public record and discussed openly.

"In contrast, drones used in non-declared combat zones do not function under explicit, public rules of engagement or chain of command. They are used covertly—meaning the government rarely acknowledges their use."[41] One informed commentator estimated by early 2012 there had been more than three hundred drone strikes outside declared war zones, with 95 percent of these being in Pakistan, resulting in deaths of more than 2,000 militants and an unknown number of civilians.[42] By the end of 2014 the BIJ claimed on its website that there had been over four hundred drone attacks in Pakistan, with total deaths in a range of 2,400 to

3,888 persons. Of those numbers the estimate of civilian deaths ranges from 416 to 959. Because the CIA, not the Pentagon, is responsible for the vast majority of these strikes, there is little firm knowledge of the actual statistics. Since the vast majority of the drone strikes in Pakistan occur in tribal areas that are outside of government control, it is very risky for Western journalists to be present. It is known that following a strike, militants in the area will seal off access, remove their dead, and permit only sympathetic local reporters to decide on a body count of casualties.[43] There must be a good measure of intellectual humility about the statistics on casualties; most of what we have constitutes educated guesses.

A figure often cited by drone critics came from David Kilcullen and Andrew McDonald Exum, who suggested the ratio was 50 civilians to 1 militant.[44] No reputable group has provided any evidence to corroborate those numbers. In fact, the data provided by the most commonly cited sources do not even remotely support the Kilcullen-Exum claims. For example, if the BIJ data for Pakistan are used and one takes the low figure for both total casualties and civilian casualties there is a ratio of 5.77 to 1. If one chooses the high figures for both groups the ratio is a fraction above 4 combatants to 1 civilian.

To illustrate the broadest possible range, however, first take the high estimate of total deaths and the low estimate of civilian deaths, producing a ratio of 9.4 combatant deaths to 1 civilian. Then taking the low estimate of total deaths and the high estimate of civilian deaths creates a ratio of 2.5 *combatants* to 1 *civilian*. While this latter figure is certainly troubling, compare it to the Kilcullen-Exum claim of a ratio of 50 *civilians* killed for every 1 *combatant* and it becomes apparent that their claim lies far outside the range of responsible estimates of civilian casualties.

At the other extreme, Obama officials have suggested that after hundreds of drone attacks the total number of civilian casualties is in the single digits. While not "empirically disproven," the government's figures are "based on deeply problematic assumptions" about the identity of those present in a strike area.[45] It has been reported that the United States views all military-age males as militants unless there is clear evidence to the contrary found in a postattack analysis. This assumption is based upon the claim that al-Qaida maintains tight operational security so anyone close to a known militant must be a militant too. Such an assumption has been challenged on several grounds. First, no person, not even a terrorist, lives in isolation. Many militants live with their families and interact with a host of others—shopkeepers, drivers, farmers, neighbors, in-laws—who are innocent civilians but who do have regular contact. Second, many of the associated forces that are treated as al-Qaida allies have lesser operational security and "denser connections with the civilian population than al-Qaida has." Thus, such low-level militants are more deeply embedded in the general noncombatant population. And finally, many of the targeted areas, such as Waziristan, function within a cultural norm that large numbers of family members live together in a single dwelling.[46] Therefore, to assume that all males in an area are active terrorists and that a known terrorist only consorts with fellow terrorists is dubious.

Recall, too, that the careful process of targeted killing presented in chapter 4 is only one way that drone strikes occur. There is the use of "double-tap" and signature strikes as well, and these greatly heighten the likelihood that civilians have been killed in U.S. drone strikes. Decisions to employ drone strikes in such circumstances, however, are policy choices and not anything inherent in the nature of attack drones.

A more sober judgment about casualties comes from a comprehensive study by Ritika Singh.[47] She correctly observes that "five studies have played perhaps the most substantial role in shaping the public debate on civilian deaths from drone strikes."[48] The NAF and the LWJ have created online databases that are regularly updated and that are cited by the media and academics. The BIJ has done similar work that challenges the lower estimates of civilian deaths found in the American reports. Two academic sources, the Columbia Law School Human Rights Clinic and the joint work of the International Human Rights and Conflict Resolution Clinic at Stanford Law School and the Global Justice Clinic at the New York University School of Law have also issued reports that are widely cited as well. The Stanford/NYU report did not give its own figures but provided a critique of the others.

What Singh has done in her "metastudy" of the casualty data is correlate the data from all these sources with attention to the different counting methods employed. There remains a fairly broad range of probable civilian casualties even after Singh's work, but if one takes the overlap between the high range of the more conservative studies and the low range of the more liberal studies the numbers look like this: Pakistan (2004–2014) has a civilian death rate of 11–15 percent of those killed by drone airstrikes, with a declining percentage in recent years. In Yemen (2002–2014) the rate is 5–18 percent. The percentage of civilian casualties is hardly negligible, but if going forward the percentage of civilian casualties were to be below 10 percent this would be a dramatic reversal of most modern wars where, according the ICRC, the percentage was almost 90 percent of casualties being civilian.

The figures, disputed as they may be, support the defenders of drones in airstrikes when they assert that drone attacks are more accurate and much less prone to cause civilian deaths than attacks from manned aircraft. This is credited to the nature of drones since their operators may observe the target longer and can use smaller munitions due to their accuracy.[49] It is certainly the case, according to their defenders, that attack drones cause fewer civilian deaths than F-16 fighter planes, B-1 bombers, or other more traditional aerial attack measures.[50] Indeed, one critic of American policy on drones has said the complaint about drones killing civilians is a "red herring," since "*every* weapons system can cause civilian casualties."[51] For supporters of drone use the telling question in the debate is not how many civilian deaths are caused by drone attacks but whether the loss of life would be greater or less were there to be aerial attacks by manned aircraft or ground troop action instead.[52] The evidence drawn from the historical record leads to the conclusion that drones allow for greater discrimination in targeting and significantly reduced civilian deaths.

In sum, there is no firm evidence that drone strikes done with careful oversight necessarily cause disproportionate civilian casualties, while the preponderance of evidence suggests that drone strikes are considerably more discriminating than older, more familiar methods of aerial assault.

And it is widely believed by those who study drone strikes that the number of unintended civilian deaths has declined steeply in recent years when compared to the early period of the Obama presidency.[53] This is not to say there have not been individual drone strikes that caused disproportionate civilian deaths, but taken as a class of actions there is nothing inherently disproportionate about drone attacks. Indeed the data suggest that drone attacks are less likely to cause civilian deaths than other weapons used in modern warfare such as cruise missiles, artillery shells, or fighter planes dropping smart bombs.[54] Again, the ICRC has concluded that armed conflicts in the twentieth century produced 1,000 civilian casualties for every 100 combatants.[55] Even a critic of the U.S. drone policy acknowledges that drone strikes kill 14 civilians for every 100 combatants. That is a dramatic change in the ratio of casualties in armed conflict.[56]

However, while determining the ratio of civilian to militant deaths is the focus of many commentators, it is not the only concern about harm to civilians. A number of studies have suggested the psychological and emotional effects upon civilian populations from drones are worrisome indeed.[57] Drones are reported to have distinct negative effects upon civilian populations. As the Stanford/NYU study documents, those living under hovering drones find their presence to be a source of terror. Daily life is affected by the ever-present buzz of drones, giving rise to constant worry about safety. Villagers worry that a strike may land in a public square, or a neighbor's home. Because of signature strikes, people shy away from gathering in groups and some parents keep their children from school.

Property loss and damage to nearby buildings resulting from a drone strike can lead to financial ruin for poor families. Injury from flying debris or the explosive force caused by a strike can harm the person who is the main source of family income. Double-tap strikes make the ordinary humane gestures of rescue and relief to victims of an earlier attack dangerous. And the covert nature of most drone strikes in Pakistan, Yemen, and Somalia means there is often no opportunity for the United States to make amends through financial compensation and other humanitarian assistance. People caught in the covert drone war have no office to contact, no process to follow that allows them to seek accountability for the harm they have suffered.[58]

There are serious social effects to the drone program. It is not just the targeted victims, but many others suffer in ways that might not come readily to mind from the safe distance of U.S. society. Often paid informants are involved in tracking targets and this has given rise to suspicion among villagers as to who might be passing along information about oneself or others to the Americans. If an attack goes awry, causing death, physical injury, or material damage, a good deal of resentment results between those who have suffered and those looked upon as possible informants. Many of the social ties that make life in a small village pleasant can be undermined as a consequence of the presence of drones in the skies over northern Pakistan and in Yemen.[59]

The nonlethal harm to civilians in areas where drone attacks occur is rarely given the coverage it deserves. If it were, there might be less confidence that drone strikes are as surgically clean as some people believe. The civilian victims of drones are not only those who have died but those who live with physical injury, economic harm, and psychological trauma. Of course this has always been an aspect of war's evil. There are many evils besides death brought on by armed conflict. Drone strikes are not innocent of those evils. Yet, when examined comparatively with other means of violence, it remains likely that attack drones allow for greater discrimination and proportionality than other methods of combat.

LAST RESORT

Classically the criterion of last resort referred to the genuine effort to find alternatives to violence and the employment of it only when all other reasonable options were foreclosed. In the present discussion that understanding is still relevant, but it is broadened to include a concern with how drone strikes may be such an attractive choice for policymakers that their availability will make war too easy.[60] The concern takes four forms. The first suggests that drones have been developed not to protect civilians better but to wage war where we otherwise would not.[61] Drones make the use of force possible where it would not have been feasible in the past.[62] Consequently, there is not a net saving of lives, even if the weapons are more discriminating by the standards of just war thinking.

The second way that the relative ease of drone warfare raises a concern has to do with the judgment about feasibility of capture rather than use of a lethal drone strike. Because drones permit killing with very little risk to American lives and a capture operation will always entail some degree of risk, do drones change the judgment of feasibility? The Obama administration has never stated what degree of risk the military should be willing to accept before it declares capture and arrest to be unfeasible. The concern is that killing may become not a last resort but the preferred option in the struggle against terrorism. The ratio of kills to arrests in recent years would suggest that there is reason to worry that the ease of resorting to drone strikes may be swaying the calculus of national leaders who are always anxious about American casualties.[63]

Because drones have proven so attractive to political leaders as a way to project armed force, there is a risk that the moral criteria of the just war tradition will be loosely interpreted so as to be able to employ drone strikes more often. An example of this danger is the relaxation of the norm of discrimination with the adoption of the policy of presuming that all MAMs in a kill zone are combatants.

A fourth form that the concern about ease of drone use takes is that the lowering of risk to the U.S. military may translate into making resort to war more likely.[64] The reasoning is that policymakers engage in careful determinations before committing to the use of armed force. Part of the calculation by a nation's leadership is the cost in American lives. The anticipation of significant loss of life deters a rash decision. When there is little risk to American lives, a major worry is removed from the decision-making process. As Benjamin Friedman puts it, "free wars are more likely to be dumb wars." That does not mean we want to put our troops in harm's way, but we ought to remember a fundamental axiom of orthodox price theory: if you lower cost you increase demand. One of the key restraints on rash resort to violence is the suffering and death that it entails for one's own military.[65] It is conceivable that drones may weaken that restraint as ease of use tempts policymakers to overuse them. The worry is that, given the relatively low cost in money and risk to the American military, our political leaders will be tempted to use drones to excess.

A related line of criticism underscores the point that if the criterion of last resort recedes in importance, there can be a skewing of the policy on counterterrorism. A comprehensive approach to counterterrorism will have many elements, only one of which is the employment of armed force. Has the balance been struck properly between the use of armed drones and other tactics in the struggle against terrorists? Or has the option that ought to be the last resort become so readily available that reliance upon it has led to underappreciating other approaches that should precede violence?

The concern is well put by the Center for Civilians in Conflict: "if U.S. use of force through drone strikes becomes unexceptional, it risks displacing alternative and non-lethal approaches to counterterrorism, such as intelligence-gathering and investigation, detention by the U.S. or partner governments, and preventive measures to stem extremism and militancy."[66] Indeed, it is reported that then Secretary of State Hillary Clinton and other major administration figures expressed concerns about a "drones-only approach" that focused on the pros and cons of a particular strike and that shortchanged other necessary components of an effective counterterrorism strategy.[67]

The criterion of last resort can be met even when the concerns noted above are taken seriously. It is possible for there to be legitimate acts of targeted killing using drones. The question is whether U.S. counterterrorism policy is too narrowly focused on drone strikes to the detriment of the overall struggle against counterterrorism. Are other dimensions necessary for a successful approach to counterterrorism being neglected? Surely the CIA's heavy involvement in drone attacks and targeted killing distracts attention and diverts resources from its fundamental mission of gathering intelligence. An effective counterterrorism policy ought to employ nonmilitary resources to engage in peacebuilding through respect for human rights, providing education, and addressing injustices that radicalize people. It is unclear whether such measures are receiving their due if top policymakers become too concentrated on the use of drones for targeted killing.

The danger that armed force will play too large a part in an overall strategy and no longer be used as a last resort leads to a related concern about armed drones, one that has to do with the relationship between the tactic of drone strikes and the strategy of counterterrorism.

STRATEGIC SUCCESS

Most theories of just war include a norm concerned with the probability of success in the use of force. Since lethal violence is such an evil, it cannot be employed without good reason, and the fruitless or ineffective pursuit of a goal hardly suffices for such a reason.

At one level the use of drone attacks in targeted killing appears to be very successful. If the point of the policy was to cripple and eliminate the threat of al-Qaida then much has been accomplished. A great deal of al-Qaida's infrastructure has been dismantled, many of its leaders have been killed, and locales that were sanctuaries for terrorist groups have been made inhospitable. This was done at relatively little financial cost, without significant risk to the U.S. military, and with fewer civilian casualties than alternative methods would have brought about.[68] As several defenders of targeted killing in the Israeli debate argued, a terrorist organization can be severely hampered by targeted killings of personnel possessing special skills, like bomb makers or forgers.

We know from intercepted communications that the drone program has driven many terrorists underground and has hampered their ability to train new recruits, plan new attacks, and manage operations. Much energy and time is spent in securing personal safety and not attacking others.[69] So attack drones clearly can be an effective measure for disrupting terrorist networks. Without question, armed drones have been tactically useful weapons.

Even if all that is granted, there remains a question about the role that drone strikes play in the overall effort to oppose terrorism. Drone attacks are but a part of counterterrorism strategy and this is why critics raise the question of effectiveness. Because of the success of drone strikes in dismantling al-Qaida, there is a risk of becoming overly reliant upon them. Retired general Stanley McChrystal has spoken of "counterinsurgency math." If you eliminate two bad guys, how many are left? The answer is, maybe more than before, because each individual has a father, a brother, a son, a friend, a fellow tribesman who now is a potential enemy. And if that was the case with killing counterinsurgents, how much more is it the case with civilian casualties? Has the administration really weighed this calculus sufficiently in our policy? The United States is not held blameless when civilians die and that harms our overall approach. Is the tactic of drone strikes undercutting the possibility for success in the comprehensive strategy to combat terrorists?[70]

In its report the Stimson Center Task Force observed that the terrorists hunted by drone operators "are often mostly motivated by localized conflicts occurring in states with fractured political orders. The use of UAVs to track and kill such individuals does not repair the political rifts that give rise to terrorist violence."[71] In another study, done by the Rand Corporation, more than 250 terrorist organizations operating during the timeframe between 1968 and 2006 were examined and it was found that the two most effective ways to eliminate terrorist groups were through reaching peaceful political arrangements with governments (43 percent of the time) or by police and intelligence agencies infiltrating the groups (40 percent of the time). Reliance upon a military approach worked less than 10 percent of the time. That is not because the military effort was unsuccessful at the level of operational effectiveness. Rather, when staying in a given area becomes too difficult for terrorists, they simply move their attention to another region. This may happen in the case of Pakistan, where it is reported that terrorists have left for new struggles in Syria, Yemen, Iraq, or their homelands.[72] Military leaders working in counterinsurgency know the line, "you can't kill your way to a solution." The same insight is applicable with counterterrorism.

A study by Jenna Jordan has looked at the specific strategy of "leadership decapitation" in combating terrorism. Her sample extended to almost three hundred groups over a sixty-year period and led to the conclusion that decapitation does not lower the lifespan of a group and it is possible that it even increases a group's survival chances.[73] As Robert Wright puts it, "You might as well try to end the personal computer business by killing executives at Apple and Dell. Capitalism being the stubborn thing it is, new executives would fill the void, so long as there was a demand for computers."[74] Wright may not fully appreciate that a terrorist recruiter has a more challenging job than a corporate headhunting firm, but the data from Jordan should give us pause about what the long-term effectiveness of the drone strategy against terrorist leaders will be. Furthermore, among those terrorist groups that were markedly harmed by decapitation, they were characterized by a clear hierarchical structure, were less than a decade old, and lacked clear paths for succession. These are qualities that are quite unlike al-Qaida and some other terrorist groups.[75]

A widespread and long-standing policy of drone strikes may contribute to the persistence of terrorism by reminding people that they are subject to the power of others whom they cannot know or see. The covert nature of the CIA drone operations means there is no acknowledgment of any harm to innocent civilians and no means whereby victims can seek compensation or ask for accountability. A sense of unresponsive domination and control can foster animosity toward the power of the United States and sympathy toward those who propose striking back violently wherever American vulnerabilities can be exploited. Mark Bowden has vividly described the feeling of impotence that gives way to rage among those who survive a drone strike. How do they vent their feelings? "No army is arrayed against them; no airfield is nearby to be attacked. If they manage to shoot down a drone, what have they done but disable a small machine? No matter how justified a strike seems to us, no matter how carefully weighed and skillfully applied, to those on the receiving end it is profoundly arrogant, the act of an enemy so distant and superior that he is untouchable."[76] The disparity between the seemingly invincible power of the United States and the impotence of those still on the ground is exploited to gain support for organizations that pledge to strike back at the faceless Americans.

Certainly the Taliban, al-Qaida, and other terrorist associations have used drone strikes as a recruiting tool and as a way to stoke anti-American sentiment among Pakistanis and others. There is a concern that the "drone strikes in Yemen risk turning 'Yemeni militants with strictly local agendas . . . [into] dedicated enemies of the West in response to U.S. military actions'" aimed at them.[77] This undercuts the larger counterterrorism strategy of gaining support from the local population and discouraging people from siding with terrorist groups.[78] The unwise lack of transparency in the Obama administration's use of covert CIA operations also hampers the effort in this area. Drone strikes are considerably less deadly and more discriminating than the propaganda organs of terrorism claim, but the United States does not successfully rebut the claims of groups like As Shab, the propaganda arm of al-Qaida that has skillfully framed "Americans as moral bullies" on the Internet.[79]

Drone strikes have also caused a backlash against the United States in countries that are not directly affected by such strikes. Some of this is due to the successful public relations campaigns waged by militants that exploit allegations of excessive civilian casualties among fellow Muslims. There are other factors as well, including concerns over sovereignty, transparency, accountability, and other rule of law issues between nations. Many political leaders, intellectuals, and shapers of public opinion even in allied nations have questioned the U.S. drone policy. If, as Obama administration officials argue, the criticisms are founded on erroneous information, there is still a price to pay when normally allied partners criticize the United States. That price might include an unwillingness to allow American bases that launch drones to operate within a nation, pressure on national leaders not to share intelligence with the United States, or less cooperation in diplomatic initiatives for fear of seeming to be too identified with U.S. policies.[80]

In congressional testimony given on April 23, 2013, international lawyer Rosa Brooks talked about the "true costs" of the American drone policy. She cited the consensus among experts in counterterrorism that "terrorist organizations are rarely defeated militarily." More commonly "terrorist groups fade away when they lose the support of the populations within which they work. They die out when their ideological underpinnings come undone—when new recruits stop appearing—when the communities in which they work stop providing active or passive forms of assistance." Brooks noted that a truly comprehensive strategy for counterterrorism takes this into account and "relies heavily on activities intended to undermine terrorist credibility within populations, as well as on activities intended to disrupt terrorist communications and financing." Without denying there is a role for military action, including targeted killing using drones, Brooks expressed concern that the Obama administration had come to define the effectiveness of the drone policy too narrowly. "[I]t is hard not to wonder whether we have begun to trade tactical gains for strategic losses."[81]

Other commentators also have expressed concern with the emphasis that has been given to drone strikes within counterterrorism planning. It should be noted that much of the criticism focuses on the CIA-run covert program outside the battle zones of Iraq and Afghanistan, namely, the drone strikes in Pakistan, Yemen, and Somalia. The reservations about the prominence of attack drones have three main aspects. First, the drone program helps to create new recruits for Islamic militant groups. Second, it fosters anti-American sentiment in targeted countries and around the wider world, making cooperation with the United States harder for other national governments. Third, the drone strikes "corrode the stability and legitimacy of local governments."[82] We have touched upon the first two points already, but the last criticism deserves additional comment.

Essentially, the charge is that the U.S. drone policy works "at cross purposes with many other U.S. counterterrorism objectives."[83] Both the Bush and Obama administrations maintain that the terrorist threat is greatly abetted by the reality of regions around the world where effective government does not exist and terrorists can operate with little concern for the rule of law. As with the declared war zones of Afghanistan and Iraq, so too with Pakistan, Yemen, and Somalia where the aim is to help the national governments attain a measure of control and efficacy in establishing jurisdiction by the central government over the regions within their borders that are presently ungoverned. That entails helping these central governments gain a sense of legitimacy from the regional populations and draw loyalty away from terror organizations, tribal groups, and local militias.

In Pakistan the perception that the government is incapable of stopping drone attacks within its borders undermines the prestige and legitimacy of the Islamabad regime. Such perceived weakness opens the central government to scorn and criticism from domestic groups opposed to the national government. It makes it increasingly difficult for the United States to assist in building Islamabad's capacity for governance when the United States regularly ignores the popular calls to respect Pakistan's sovereignty.[84] The extent of the CIA program has put the United States in the center of the struggle within the tribal region and made the Islamabad government appear to be marginal. That hurts the effort to enhance the role of the central government in previously ungovernable locales.

A similar claim can be made concerning Yemen, where there is growing evidence that the United States had been targeting not global terrorist networks but local insurgents who were focused on opposition to the present regime. Many of the drone strikes were not aimed at al-Qaida in the Arabian Peninsula but people hostile to the government.[85] By expanding the number of drone strikes, the United States was taking sides in a conflict where it is unclear if global terror that threatens the United States is the real issue. And by so manifestly propping up the government in Sana'a, the United States radicalized opposition to the central government as being illegitimate and beholden to American power.

Without question there are benefits to targeted killings using drones in the struggle against terrorists. Many critics of the policy who are included here do not deny that is the case. To varying degrees, however, they express a concern that the policy looms too large as a component of the counterterrorism strategy of the United States and that the drone attacks "overshadow and diminish the effectiveness of civilian assistance programs."[86] Lethal violence can be justified in attacking global terror networks, but it cannot be the sum of the tools employed or even the top priority in counterterrorism.

PERPETUAL WAR

Yet another concern about the frequent use of drone strikes is that they "may create a slippery slope" that leads to continual war. The relatively low cost and low risk to the American military of drone warfare could encourage the pursuit of targets "that would be deemed not worth pursuing if manned aircraft or special operations forces had to be put at risk."[87] In the past the presence of risk has served to restrain the use of armed force that is unnecessary to the completion of the United States' goals. By significantly diminishing the risk of losing American lives, drones make resort to force more appealing even if not strictly necessary. As a supporter of drone attacks warns, "the U.S. government needs to remember that many of the world's jihadist organizations are focused first and foremost on local regimes and that although the United States has an interest in helping its allies fight extremists, Washington cannot and should not directly involve itself in every fight."[88]

It appears that the effectiveness of drone strikes in carrying out targeted killings against leaders of al-Qaida and other global terrorist networks has morphed more and more into a wider attack upon targets that cannot be described as HVTs or as posing a serious threat to the United States. The Obama administration has expanded targeted killing to a scale where now most of those being killed are low-ranking foot soldiers. It has been widely reported that the overwhelming majority of victims of drone strikes are not HVTs and that even with the increasing reliance upon drones the number of HVT deaths has not increased.[89] In a number of cases the United States relied upon intelligence reports from other countries that led to American drones being used to kill people who were dubious as threats to us but who were out of favor with a foreign intelligence agency.[90] As Audrey Kurth Cronin has written, we should make sure that "local insurgencies remain local" and then use "drones rarely, selectively, transparently, and only against those who can realistically target the United States." We are too close to an era in which the Obama administration "finds itself in a permanent battle with an amorphous and geographically dispersed foe, one with an increasingly marginal connection to the original 9/11 plotters."[91]

Already in the short period of the Obama administration there has been a dramatic change in the use of drones. Drone strikes have gone from a military weapon used in a narrow range of situations for specifically targeted individuals who were high-ranking figures in al-Qaida to a weapon used in a growing number of countries to kill a lengthening list of people. Only some of those targeted went through the process of being named on a kill list, and many of them were unlikely to participate in international terrorism against the United States.[92] The result is a growing risk that the United States will find itself in a state of perpetual war with radicalized Islamists. Sadly, there is no evident end to this state of affairs, but rather "an endless cycle of perceived threat, drone strikes, inevitable collateral damage, and mutual animosity."[93]

BAD PRECEDENTS

> From the perspective of many around the world, the United States currently appears to claim, in effect, the legal right to kill any person it determines is a member of al-Qaida or its associated forces, in any state on Earth, at any time, based on secret criteria and secret evidence, evaluated in a secret process by unknown and largely anonymous individuals—with no public disclosure of which organizations are considered "associated forces" (or how combatant status is determined or how the United States defines "participation in hostilities"), no means for anyone outside the secret process to raise questions about the criteria or validity of the evidence, and no means for anyone outside that process to identify or remedy mistakes or abuses.[94]

That harsh description is not taken from a document written by a sworn enemy of the United States or published on the website of an organization with a deep anti-American animus. It is an excerpt from the executive summary of a report that was produced by a task force cochaired by a retired general and former head of the U.S. Central Command. The task force was composed of former military personnel, national security policymakers, and international lawyers well known in Washington. It should be noted the report does not endorse all these indictments against U.S. policy but it does take seriously the perception by others that the allegations are accurate.

Those allegations include violation of the international norm of sovereignty, a lack of transparency regarding the criteria for targeting, the absence of any appeal mechanism or external means for evaluation of U.S. actions, and no apparent process for determining accountability or rectifying errors when they occur. The United States sees itself as a leader of the global community. It should exercise that leadership by advancing international norms to govern the standards and restrictions for drone use.

A frequent lament among critics is that the Obama administration has missed an opportunity regarding the setting of precedents for drone use. "History shows that how states adopt and use new military capabilities is often influenced by how other states have—or have not—used them in the past."[95] For example, biological and chemical weapons, as well as landmines and blinding lasers, have all been employed far less than they might have been had there not been efforts to establish norms, sometimes through legal regimes, to dissuade nations from using them. Furthermore, norms can even deter states from acquiring new technologies.

Richard Haass maintains that the Obama administration should be actively working to make drone strikes the exception rather than the new norm for dealing with terrorists.[96] Peter Singer and Thomas Wright recall the era when the United States helped set nuclear doctrine and have urged President Obama to do something similar at the onset of the drone era. America should outline the framework that will guide the development, deployment, and use of drones. By going public with its own drone doctrine, the hope would be for the United States to shape the strategic environment in which other nations think about drones.[97]

This concern about precedents may seem to some to be naive, given the way that the laws of war are often neglected. It is true that rules get violated in every field of endeavor, but it is rules that make it possible to criticize the violators. "If the U.S. were to firmly establish high standards for the use of armed drones, then even if a rogue country did not adhere to the standards the international security situation would likely be improved, with other nations more likely to rally against the rogue nation."[98]

For the United States to maintain its claim to global leadership, it is insufficient to maintain its military and economic preeminence. There are also political and moral dimensions to the American conviction of its leadership role. For the sake of that moral leadership the government should proclaim and abide by a code of behavior for drone warfare. A major part of that code should reflect discrimination (e.g., genuine precision in targeting) and proportionality (e.g., not going after a low-level militant whenever collateral damage is likely). These norms should be clear and people should be held accountable when the norms are violated. Concern for setting precedents will require a dramatic change in the existing way in which the administration operates—relying upon classified memoranda and too little public discussion about the legal, strategic, and ethical architecture that supports American drone policy. Yet "without reform from within, drones risk becoming an unregulated, unaccountable vehicle for states to deploy lethal force with impunity."[99]

Without question other nations will obtain armed drones and use them in ways that are not in accord with U.S. interests. The process of intentionally setting precedents for the future ought to lead to rethinking present and past policies so that a coming world where attack drones are no longer in the hands of the United States alone will be a world of order and security for all people.

One important precedent concerns striking the appropriate balance between fighting transnational terrorism and the traditional norm of sovereignty. Drones represent a technology with the potential to undercut the idea of national sovereignty. According to existing international norms a state may utilize armed force within another state's borders in three circumstances: first, if a state consents to the other state's action; second, when the UN Security Council authorizes the intervention; and the third circumstance is when armed force is used in accord with a nation's right of self-defense against attack.

President Obama has largely eschewed the Bush administration's language of a global war on terror. Nonetheless, his employment of the language of self-defense allows him to attain the same goal, which is to use drones in regions that were not part of the acknowledged battle zones of Iraq and Afghanistan. According to the Justice Department, the targeted killings carried out by drone strikes are not violations of another state's sovereignty if that state consents or if it is "unwilling or unable" to stop the threat posed by the individual or group being targeted. At first glance that statement is not an extreme or outlandish claim for a government to make. The difficulty with it becomes clearer once it is realized that the only one who will determine whether a state is "unwilling or unable" to deal with the alleged threat is the Obama administration. There is a circular argument at the core of the present drone policy.

Once the United States decides that a resident of another country is a legitimate target on the grounds of self-defense due to the threat the person poses to Americans, there are two options. One is that the country consents to let the United States strike, which resolves the sovereignty issue. Alternatively, the country does not agree with the U.S. proposal. Then the Obama administration simply concludes the other country is an unwilling partner in the fight against global terror and therefore goes ahead with the targeted killing using an armed drone.

As Rosa Brooks concludes, "this is a legal theory that more or less eviscerates traditional notions of sovereignty" and will serve to destabilize the already shaky edifice of collective security erected by the UN Charter. "If the U.S. is the sole arbiter of whether and when it can use force inside the borders of another state, any other state strong enough to get away with it is likely to claim similar prerogatives."[100] Recall, as well, that the executive branch is also the sole arbiter of who is a legitimate target and what makes a threat imminent and it becomes apparent that such a policy precedent will permit many other nations to justify a host of targeted killings. The erosion of the norm of sovereignty through the use of force when a nation's consent is questionable or nonexistent will only encourage others to do similar acts, thereby increasing the danger of more conflicts around the globe.[101]

In the world of bioethics there has long been a warning to avoid what has been called the "technological imperative," the idea that because we have the means to do something we ought to do it. Opponents of such technological determinism have argued that technology must be subject to wise and humane guidance. For example, not everything that can be done in genetic engineering or in the use of life-extending procedures automatically serves human flourishing. There is the distinct possibility that in the realm of counterterrorism we are allowing a technological imperative to drive our strategy rather than the reverse. Because we have the wherewithal to use drones to attack targeted individuals and groups in locales not readily accessible to other forms of intervention does not mean we should do so. It is important that we pause to consider the impact upon global order if we become cavalier about the norms of territorial integrity and political sovereignty as a consequence of our use of drones.

Obviously, lethal drones also are capable of undermining the international standard prohibiting assassination. Individuals residing in one state could be killed by a foreign government if they are deemed a threat, without that government having to declare war. A government might define a threat to be global terrorists, as the United States presently claims, but other alleged threats could be spies, expatriate dissidents, intellectuals, or journalists. Indeed, a threat could be just about anyone declared so by a government. The question, therefore, is whether the Obama administration is "inadvertently handing abusive foreign regimes a playbook for murdering those it considers politically inconvenient, under the guise of combatting terrorism."[102] There is the danger that a bad precedent for armed drones could create "a world where states can increasingly take vengeance on individuals outside their borders without the niceties of extradition, due process or trial."[103]

Another dangerous precedent concerns the issue of targeted killing beyond a declared zone of hostilities. On a traditional battlefield the targeting of combatants is uncontroversial. Drone strikes in Afghanistan or Iraq clearly were used as part of counterinsurgency warfare, even if there were some attacks that were disproportionate or insufficiently discriminate. The far more controversial use of drones is in Pakistan, Yemen, and Somalia as part of counterterrorism policy. Here the issue is determining who is a combatant engaged in terrorist activity. Critics, as we have seen, maintain that the United States has targeted individuals and groups for drone strikes without sufficient reason. The critics have also charged that drone strikes have occurred in places that do not qualify as legitimate fields of combat.

Expanding the conflict with al-Qaida and its associated groups beyond Afghanistan and Iraq has led to criticism that the United States is acting as if the laws of war can be stretched to apply in every place. For one critic the U.S. policy means "we have a global battlefield, which completely undercuts any possibility of talking about just war. There are no boundaries to this thing."[104] Extending the battlefield to include everywhere sets a precedent that puts everyone at risk of being in the wrong place at the wrong time.

Other voices make related criticisms. Kenneth Roth argues that when away from the battlefield it is not international humanitarian law, the special law of war, that should govern U.S. actions. That means arrest would be the norm, not targeted killing, when people are identified as terrorists. As was noted above, when using drones the United States has gone after armed groups in Yemen and Somalia that may have far more to do with insurgent opposition to those local governments than any terror threat to the United States.[105] William Pfaff wonders who decided that the United States is to be the global police force intervening across borders when there is no demonstrable threat to American national security and those targeted had no involvement in 9/11. For Pfaff we have moved into an undefined state of armed conflict that both feeds and reflects a foolish sense of a "clash of civilizations."[106]

The danger, cited by those who fear the extension of drone strikes beyond defined battlefields, is what precedent this will establish for other nations as they develop armed drones. Will Russia feel free to attack alleged Chechen "combatants" throughout Europe, or might China kill

Uighur "combatants" in the United States?[107] Similarly, Robert Wright charges, the United States is stating, "it's OK to lob missiles into countries that haven't attacked you, as long as you think a terrorist may live there. Do we really want to send that message to, for example, Russia and China, both of which have terrorism problems? Or India? Or Pakistan?"[108]

Although there is rhetorical force in these questions, they pose a rather unlikely scenario in one sense. Recall that drones fly low and slow and are noisy. They are not practical weapons unless their operators control the airspace. Any nation with sophisticated air defense systems can protect itself from drone attacks. As Bowden notes, drones are "only slightly harder to shoot down than a hot-air balloon."[109] So the risk of a precedent that will threaten residents in nations with advanced air defenses is small.

What that suggests, of course, is while developed nations will not have to fear drone strikes over their territory, poorer nations may be readily subjected to such external interventions. This will only further antagonize masses of people and convince them that the rules of international order are set by the powerful for the powerful. That, in turn, will promote awareness of the disparities of power between nations like the United States and those where terrorists find support. Such awareness will only add to the numbers of those opposing American interests.

As U.S. drone strikes increase in number, and as the proliferation of armed drones becomes ever more likely, it is imperative that attention be given to how widespread and regular use of such weapons will affect the lives of ordinary people as they go about their lives in areas previously presumed to be safe from attack. Perhaps what is needed is the creation by executive order of a nonpartisan, independent commission to review targeted killings outside declared battlefields. The commission members should reflect diversity and be persons with unquestionable credibility. They would have no role in the process before a strike but be assigned the task of reviewing the policy and the approval process for such strikes both by the military and the CIA. They should also publish unclassified versions of the reports submitted to the president and congressional oversight committees about their findings.[110] Turning every locale of some nations into a possible target area does not seem to be a sensible way to restrain resorting to armed force. A different precedent ought to be the legacy of U.S. policy, one that clarifies the moral and legal norms for drone strikes outside declared battlefields.

Thus far we have discussed a variety of concerns about existing American policy on the use of drones in targeted killing. There remains still another important concern to be touched upon and it has to do with the way that the existing drone policy affects the nature of a democratic polity.

DRONES AND DEMOCRACY

Few things unite critics of drone strikes more than the charge that there is a serious lack of transparency and accountability surrounding the American policy and the use of drones in targeted killing. Responsible critics acknowledge there is a degree of secrecy necessary in counterterrorism, but they argue that in a democracy it remains important that there be public discussion of the moral and strategic issues involved in the government's program of using drones for targeted killing. Operational secrecy should not mean transparency, accountability, and oversight of the executive branch's actions are taken out of democratic life.

Historically, the decision to use military force was a choice made by elected representatives. It was one way that the American people could be engaged, through congressional debate, in the judgment to go to war, and so be willing to bear its burdens through paying the expenses and mustering adequate personnel. The drafters of the Constitution intentionally separated the president's role as commander in chief from Congress's role in declaring a war.

Troubling is that the technological advances of armed drones are "short-circuiting the decision-making process" by American democracy. Because of the ready availability of armed drones to support a targeted killing policy, "something that would have previously been viewed as a war is simply not being treated like a war."[111] For example, the White House never sought congressional approval of its role in the air war over

Libya during 2011. There were more than 146 offensive strikes carried out by unmanned vehicles over six months, but Congress was never asked to vote on the action. The administration stated that since there were no ground troops and no real risk of any American casualties there was no need to seek approval from the legislative branch.

During the Libyan conflict one American vehicle was shot down. Had there been a loss of American lives or if American combatants had been taken captive there would have been a predictable call to end the operation and bring our troops home. Because the vehicle was unmanned there was hardly any public awareness of the incident. Yet when President Obama sent a small force of Special Operations troops in a noncombat role to Uganda the White House informed Congress in accordance with the War Powers Resolution.

It would seem that the new standard is that "presidents need to seek approval only for operations that send people into harm's way—not for those that involve waging war by other means."[112] And the problem is not simply executive branch activity but legislative branch inactivity. Despite ten years of extra-battlefield targeted killings, no congressional committee has conducted a hearing on the phenomenon.

If one looks at public opinion polls it is evident that the use of drone strikes in counterterrorism is overwhelmingly endorsed.[113] So it could be said that the people have spoken and there is little reason to question the administration's policy. There is also the fact that President Obama was reelected and that during the campaign neither his opponent nor the American press showed much interest in questioning the drone policy. And yet this may only demonstrate what one writer has called "a troubling, even obscene disconnect between the American people and the wars waged in our name."[114] Many observers have commented upon the distance between the American people and the military who fight on our behalf.[115] The protracted wars in Afghanistan and Iraq, along with the "war on terror," have gone on while in the meantime "most Americans have hardly felt a thing."[116] We have been a nation at war for well over a decade but this has been done with few warriors. At no point during the wars in both Iraq and Afghanistan were there ever more than three-quarters of 1 percent of the American population serving in the military. Nor were citizens even asked to finance the wars as the costs were taken off the books and the national debt grew while no tax or other sacrifice was imposed to pay for the armed conflicts. Armed drones represent the growing tendency of Americans "to let someone or something else bear the brunt of our wars." They are the ideal weapons that lower the risk of American casualties and require a modest amount of personnel to employ them. However, there remains the lurking anxiety that there is a major risk to a democracy when its citizens remain "so aloof from the wars it fights."[117]

Public opinion is a shifting reality and there have been dramatic reversals in opinion polls about military action when the media provides extensive coverage of casualties, including video and still pictures of the devastation wrought by violence. The standard for what is acceptable collateral damage is also a shifting reality; it has evolved in both stricter and looser ways during various conflicts. At present the general public in the United States is formulating its judgments about the nation's drone policy "despite the informational black hole that surrounds it."[118] Perhaps more information would lead to greater empathy for those innocents affected by drone strikes as well as more appreciation for the troublesome aspects of the overall policy.

Kenneth Roth complains about the "deliberate ambiguity" of the Obama administration's explanation regarding the legal foundation for its drone use. Lincoln Caplan comments, "Democracy works best when the government minimizes secrecy, including by recognizing that while the mechanics of national security operations must of course remain covert, there's no reason not to openly explain the *legal basis* for these operations." Americans should have learned that from the Bush administration's secret law allowing for the torture of detainees. Singer and Wright express concern that the articulation of Obama's strategic vision for the new generation of weapons has been "disjointed and preliminary." And Jesselyn Radack has charged that the "administration's position has little to do with transparency and everything to do with releasing information when politically advantageous while keeping potentially controversial or embarrassing information secret."[119]

Radack quotes a *New York Times* op-ed accusing the CIA of abusing the Glomar legal doctrine, which allows government agencies to refuse to confirm the existence of records requested under the Freedom of Information Act.[120] Without denying that the doctrine may serve a legitimate purpose, the authors of the op-ed allege that the CIA has "grossly abused" it in regard to counterterrorism operations. They charge Glomar has not been cited to preserve secrecy, given the official statements on and off the record, but to manipulate the ability of the public to make informed judgments about their government's policies.

Despite the public statements by the president and other members of the national security team, the American public still knows very little about the policy enacted in its name. For example, is there a designated devil's advocate to make the case against a specific killing? What is the level of proof demanded when determining the person ought to be targeted: beyond a reasonable doubt? By a preponderance of evidence? Reasonable suspicion?[121] The latter was supposedly the level at which the standard was set by the end of the Bush administration. The Obama administration now claims to abide by the strictest standard of beyond a reasonable doubt.

Meaningful transparency demands that there be disclosure of the policy standards, the legal justification, and those procedures in place when a decision is made to authorize a drone strike. The requirement is not that there be public approval of every targeted killing at the moment of launch, but that there be adequate information about, and oversight of, the decision-making process leading to the addition of a name to a kill list. As a general rule there should be acknowledgment after the fact that a strike took place as well as the general location of the attack and number of weapons launched. There should also be provision of basic information about the results of any strikes: Was the intended target killed? Were there other casualties? How many? Is it determined whether they were civilian or combatant? On what basis was the determination made?[122] Without such basic and essential information the citizenry cannot be informed and a democratic government undercuts the legitimacy of its own actions if it regularly and consistently refuses to provide the means whereby citizens can assess the nation's policies and determine whether to support or oppose them.

Since the administration claims the drone program already entails extensive preparation and a searching review with broad consultation on a regular basis regarding the kill lists, the call for more transparency should not cause a disruption of the timeline for decisions.[123] And unilateral executive action remains possible when there are "exigent circumstances" if accompanied by judicial review *post factum*.[124] With that set of premises it is reasonable to conclude that increased transparency will not entail placing undue restrictions that hinder effective military action. Hence, it can be concluded that the plea for improved transparency ought not be dismissed.

The announcement by the president that most of the responsibility for drone operations eventually will be shifted from the CIA to the military holds out a promise of marginal improvement in transparency. Nonetheless, since the vast majority of nonbattlefield strikes have taken place in Pakistan under the CIA's authority, it is not reassuring that those operations shall continue. The administration needs to set forth a clear policy on targeted killing in nonbattlefield regions and then demonstrate that it can hold itself accountable. By law the government cannot acknowledge covert actions undertaken by the CIA. For the sake of greater transparency, therefore, such strikes should be placed under the military's chain of command.

The parallel programs of the military and the CIA are unnecessarily "duplicative and inefficient."[125] The dual programs also make oversight by Congress more difficult. "The two organizations have different authorities, policies, accountability mechanisms, and oversight."[126] Regarding oversight the focus should not be solely on legal compliance but also include evaluation and assessment of whether the drone strike program is effectively aligned with the wider strategic objectives of counterterrorism policy. Moving the targeted killing program into the military will also permit the CIA to return to its core mission of intelligence and away from the paramilitary operations it took on after 9/11. "The United States should have a single integrated system for carrying out lethal targeted strikes outside hot battlefields." The CIA ought to continue to provide intelligence and analysis to assist in targeting, but the actual command and control of the targeted killing operation should be given over to the military.[127]

The main reason why the CIA operations have continued is to provide "plausible deniability" to the Obama administration. However, given the wide reporting of drone strikes in Pakistan, Yemen, and Somalia and the fact that only the United States has the capability of launching such attacks, there is no advantage to maintaining such unacknowledged attacks. In fact, such secrecy hinders the counterterrorism effort since it permits militants to use propaganda about the strikes while the United States cannot respond with information that could rebut the militants' claims.

If there were more transparency about our targeted killing policy and program that would also allow for improvement on the matter of accountability. As citizens we do not know what happens in poststrike assessments: Who is involved? Were mistakes made? What penalties exist for making mistakes? Have there been chronic failures in target identification? In the execution of a targeted killing?

The American system of checks and balances among three branches of government suggests the utility of some possible role for judicial input. This is not a proposal for a FISA-like court that would approve targeted killing attacks in advance.[128] There are constitutional issues that complicate introducing the judicial branch into decisions about targeting or approving an actual drone strike. These are properly military decisions. A president can delegate authority within his chain of command, but a president cannot give away his authority as commander in chief to another branch of government, nor can Congress take it away. Rather, what might be done is to have an independent review by retired judges of failed or controversial attacks to determine responsibility and culpability. It would be a process for poststrike assessment, not prestrike approval. This court could also hear grievances from victims' families and others who suffered damage from a U.S. attack.

The problem we face with the present situation is, as Senator Angus King (I-ME) has stated, that the executive functions as prosecutor, judge, jury, and executioner all in one. As Jeh Johnson, a former Pentagon lawyer, put it, "the American public is suspicious of executive power shrouded in secrecy."[129] What the American government needs is a new policy framework that defines the scope of war, enumerates the authority and the limits on presidential power, and puts in place mechanisms for review and accountability of presidential action. There ought also to be specific measures outlined whereby the president will keep the American public informed of covert activities. There should also be a set term at the end of which Congress would have to debate and vote again on whether to renew the framework.[130] Such reforms may assist in putting the counterterrorism policy of the United States within a structure with greater transparency and accountability. Most importantly, what is needed is to make sure that the methods we employ to fight terrorists do not undermine the democratic ethos of the nation.

FINAL THOUGHTS

A consequence, partially due to the impact of drones upon the consciousness of many people in the Near and Middle East, is the image of the United States as a nation with a violent and harmful approach to dealing with other peoples. The lack of transparency regarding the use of drones has been an international public relations nightmare for the United States. If part of the struggle against terrorism is to provide people with an alternative approach to the lawlessness and violence of terrorists, then the cause is not being dramatically helped by our present policy regarding drones. This may come as a surprise to Americans who strongly support the idea of drone strikes in counterterrorist action. But even among our allies the view of drones is negative.[131] Public opinion can be a fickle thing and there is no suggestion that the Obama administration must now simply bend to public opinion in other nations. Still, it is instructive to know how others see us.

It may also be sobering to reflect upon our drone policy from another viewpoint, the perspective of what philosophers and theologians call virtue ethics. What kind of a people are we becoming through the wars we prosecute and the violence we inflict? Are we losing the capacity for empathy with those people who are on the other end of our drone strikes, especially the families and friends of those innocent civilians known to us only as collateral damage? Can we simply dismiss the reported evidence of how drones terrorize people living in communities subject to their presence? Have we lost hope that things can change if we were to address the root causes of conflict: the lack of justice, economic development, and participation in public life that marginalizes the masses in countries like Pakistan, Yemen, and Somalia?[132] Have we settled for managing the conflict by focusing on military security, while giving too little attention to the need for human security that addresses the needs of people caught in the conflict? These questions are not meant to indict but to invite reflection about whether our moral imaginations have been captured by a paradigm of efficiency, low risk, and success that drones represent in the minds of many Americans. It is a paradigm that overlooks the harms being inflicted upon us as a nation and upon the people where our drones strike.

For those of us who stand within the just war tradition there is an obligation to assess the *jus in bello* aspects even of those armed conflicts that satisfy the *jus ad bellum* requirements. Should one accept the rightness of the decision for the United States to initiate a military campaign against international terrorists, there still remains a judgment to be passed on the means employed in that campaign. This chapter has presented and examined many of the complaints and reservations expressed about one particular means, the use of drone strikes in targeted killing.

I have concluded that there are moral criticisms of the American policy on drone strikes that are not persuasive, or at least not fully persuasive. There are other moral criticisms, however, that do make telling points against the present policy. Signature strikes ought to be eliminated from counterterrorism strategy. The list of those considered legitimate targets for targeted killing should be limited to true HVTs engaged in ongoing plots. Both discriminate targeting and avoidance of a perpetual state of war require care in determining those liable to be attacked. The idea of imminence in determining the nature of a threat must be reexamined to ensure that it is not severed from the probability of an attack actually taking place. It is not only that civilian deaths are to be avoided, but also that the nonlethal harm inflicted upon innocent people by the use of drones must be weighed in determining the rightness of American policy. Drone attacks should not become the default choice in counterterrorism strategy but kept as a last resort. And great caution should be exercised in the way that the United States is effectively putting in place precedents that others will appeal to in their use of armed drones in the future. Finally, the policy and process for using drones in targeted killing must not undermine the vitality of America's democratic institutions and public life.

These criticisms and concerns, serious and significant as they are, do not rise to the level of an absolute proscription of drone strikes for targeted killing. Such a tactic is neither always to be permitted nor always to be opposed. Valid criticisms do challenge the present way by which drones function within our counterterrorism strategy, our democratic polity, and our broader approach to international relations. If, however, reforms occur that give proper weight to the factors discussed in this chapter, a policy of targeted killing using drones can be a morally justifiable component within a broader strategy of counterterrorism.

NOTES

1. UNDERSTANDING TARGETED KILLING AND DRONES

1. Scott Shane, "Targeted Killing Comes to Define War on Terror," *New York Times* (April 7, 2013). http://www.nytimes.com/2013/04/08/world/targeted-killing-comes-to-define-war-on-terror.html?pagewanted=all&_r=0.

2. Ibid.

3. Steven David, *Fatal Choices: Israel's Policy of Targeted Killing* (Ramat Gan, Israel: Begin-Sadat Center for Strategic Studies, 2002), 2.

4. Philip Alston, "Study on Targeted Killings," *Report of the Special Rapporteur on Extrajudicial, Summary or Arbitrary Executions*. United Nations Human Rights Council (May 28, 2010), I, 1.

5. Uri Friedman, "Targeted Killings: A Short History," *Foreign Policy* (September/October 2012), 1–6 at 3. http://foreignpolicy.com/2012/08/13/targeted-killings-a-short-history/.

6. "Named killing" and "selected killing" are other expressions found in the literature that are more descriptive than evaluative.

7. Franklin Ford, *Political Murder: From Tyrannicide to Terrorism* (Cambridge, MA: Harvard University Press, 1985). Ford's study is very informative, but unfortunately the title of the book adds to the confusion since some of the killings he discusses are not murders because they are morally defensible.

8. 1937 Convention for the Prevention and Repression of Terrorism; 1973 Convention on the Prevention and Punishment of Crimes against Internationally Protected Persons.

9. Brian Johnstone, "Political Assassination and Tyrannicide: Traditions and Contemporary Conflicts," *Studia Moralia* 41 (2003): 25–46.

10. Presidents have not always been strict adherents of their own policy, however. For example, in 1986 Ronald Reagan authorized the bombing of Muammar Qaddafi's villa after Libya was deemed to be behind the bombing of a disco in Berlin that killed U.S. soldiers. And in 1998, after the twin bombings of U.S. embassies in Sudan and Tanzania, Bill Clinton ordered a cruise missile strike on al-Qaida sites in Afghanistan and Sudan where Osama bin Laden was thought to be residing. In all such cases government spokespersons have insisted that the attacks were on facilities, not particular individuals located at the targeted sites.

11. The role of the Lutheran theologian Dietrich Bonhoeffer in one of the plots against Hitler is an example of a morally serious Christian theologian who believed the condemnation of assassination was not absolute. As a good Lutheran, Bonhoeffer thought the assassination was necessary even while he acknowledged moral guilt for his role. In short, a real Two Kingdoms conundrum.

12. Benjamin Runkle, "The Age of the Manhunt," *Foreign Policy* (May 9, 2011), 1. http://foreignpolicy.com/2011/05/09/the-age-of-the-manhunt/.

13. Jeremy Scahill, *Dirty Wars* (New York: Nation Books, 2013).

14. Runkle, "Manhunt," 3.

15. Ibid., 4.

16. Matthew Waxman, "The Targeted Killings Debate," Council on Foreign Relations (June 8, 2011), 2. http://www.cfr.org/world/targeted-killings-debate/p25230.

17. Pardiss Kebriaei, "The Targeted Killings Debate," in ibid.

18. Micah Zenko, "10 Things You Didn't Know about Drones," *Foreign Policy* (March/April 2012), 1. http://foreignpolicy.com/2012/02/27/10-things-you-didnt-know-about-drones/.

19. Ibid., 1.

20. Christian Caryl, "Predators and Robots at War," *New York Review of Books* (September 29, 2011), 3. http://www.nybooks.com/articles/archives/2011/sep/29/predators-and-robots-war/.

21. Ibid., 3.

22. Micah Zenko, *Reforming U.S. Drone Strike Policies*, Council on Foreign Relations Special Report no. 65 (January 2013), 5.

23. Joshua Foust and Ashley Boyle, "The Strategic Context of Lethal Drones" (Washington, DC: American Security Project, 2012), 6.

24. Zenko, "10 Things You Didn't Know about Drones," 2.

25. Peter Bergen and Katherine Tiedemann, "Washington's Phantom War," *Foreign Affairs* (July/August 2011), 2. http://www.foreignaffairs.com/articles/67939/peter-bergen-and-katherine-tiedemann/washingtons-phantom-war.

26. Robotic planes are on the horizon, however. See Caryl, "Predators and Robots at War," 4.

27. Dave Majumdar, "U.S. Drone Fleet at 'Breaking Point,' Air Force Says," *Daily Beast* (January 5, 2015). http://www.thedailybeast.com/articles/2015/01/04/exclusive-u-s-drone-fleet-at-breaking-point-air-force-says.html.

28. James Dao, "Drone Pilots Are Found to Get Stress Disorders Much as Those in Combat Do," *New York Times* (January 22, 2013), 1. http://www.nytimes.com/2013/02/23/us/drone-pilots-found-to-get-stress-disorders-much-as-those-in-combat-do.html.

29. Mark Jacobson, "Five Myths about Obama's Drone War," *Washington Post* (February 8, 2013), 1. http://www.washingtonpost.com/opinions/five-myths-about-obamas-drone-war/2013/02/08/c9ef3d78–708c-11e2-a050-b83a7b35c4b5_story.html.

30. Caryl, "Predators and Robots at War," 2.

31. William Pfaff, "Anonymous Murder from a Safe Distance," *Truthdig* (April 9, 2013). http://www.truthdig.com/report/item/anonymous_murder_from_a_safe_distance_20130409.

32. Timothy Reidy, "What Are Drones Doing to US?" *America* (April 2, 2013). http://americamagazine.org/content/all-things/what-are-drones-doing-us.

33. A *New York Times*/CBS News poll asked the question: "Do you favor the U.S. using unmanned aircraft or 'drones' to carry out missile attacks against suspected terrorists in foreign countries?" In addition to those in favor and those opposed, there were 6 percent with no opinion. *New York Times* (June 13, 2013).

34. The *New Yorker* writer Jane Mayer raised this point in a live chat on the ethics of drone warfare. http://jeffersonmcmahan.com/wp-content/uploads/2012/11/New-Yorker-drone.pdf.

35. Maryann Cusimano Love, "White House: Drone Program 'Legal,' 'Ethical' and 'Wise.' Is It?" *Washington Post* (February 5, 2013). http://www.washingtonpost.com/blogs/guest-voices/post/white-house-...e-is-it/2013/02/05/2777b91c-6ff1–11e2-ac36–3d8d9dcaa2e2_blog.html.

36. Peter Singer, "Finally, Obama Breaks His Silence on Drones," *Los Angeles Times* (May 23, 2013). http://articles.latimes.com/2013/may/23/opinion/la-oe-0523-singer-obama-national-security-20130523.

37. Alston, "Study on Targeted Killings," III, G, 85.

38. Caryl, "Predators and Robots at War," 7.

39. Charli Carpenter and Lina Shaikhouni, "Don't Fear the Reaper," *Foreign Policy* (June 7, 2011), 4. http://foreignpolicy.com/2011/06/07/dont-fear-the-reaper/.

40. Micah Zenko, *Reforming U.S. Drone Strike Policies*, 8.

41. Ibid., 9.

42. Bergen and Tiedemann, "Washington's Phantom War," 1.

2. THE DISTANT CONTEXTS OF THE DEBATE

1. Franklin Ford, *Political Murder: From Tyrannicide to Terrorism* (Cambridge, MA: Harvard University Press, 1985), 2.

2. Aristotle, *Politics*, Bk. I, 5, in *The Politics and the Constitution of Athens* (Cambridge Texts in the History of Political Thought), ed. Stephen Everson (Cambridge: Cambridge University Press, 1996).

3. Ibid., III, 6.

4. Ibid., III, 7.

5. Ford, *Political Murder*, 2.

6. Ibid., 46 (italics in original).

7. Cicero, *On Duties*, Bk. III, 19 (Cambridge Texts in the History of Political Thought), ed. M. T. Griffin and E. M. Atkins (Cambridge: Cambridge University Press, 1991).

8. Ibid., Book III, 19, 32, 82–85.

9. Ford, *Political Murder*, 65.

10. The narrative of both Caesar's and Cicero's deaths can be found in Ford, *Political Murder*, 59–67.

11. Ibid., 72.

12. Ibid., 91.

13. Judges 3:12–30.

14. Judges 4:1–22.

15. Judges 5:24–27.

16. Leslie Hoppe, "Introduction to the Book of Judith," in *The Catholic Study Bible*, ed. Donald Senior (New York: Oxford University Press, 1990), 520.

17. Judges 8:29–9:56.

18. For an overview of the relationship of Jesus and his early disciples to the worldly politics of his time, see Kenneth Himes, *Christianity and the Political Order* (Maryknoll, NY: Orbis Books, 2013), chap. 3.

19. Reported in Ford, *Political Murder*, 121.

20. *The Ecclesiastical History of Sozomen*, Bk. VI, chap. 2, in *A Selected Library of Nicene and Post-Nicene Fathers of the Christian Church*, 2nd Series, ed. Philip Schaff and Henry Wace, vol. 2 (Grand Rapids, MI: Eerdmans, 1983), 346, as cited in Brian Johnstone, "Political Assassination and Tyrannicide: Tradition and Contemporary Conflicts," *Studia Moralia* 41 (2003): 25–46.

21. Augustine, *The City of God*, Bk. V, chap. 19.

22. John of Salisbury, *Policraticus*, Bk. VIII, chaps. 18, 20 in *From Irenaeus to Grotius: A Sourcebook in Christian Political Thought*, ed. Oliver O'Donovan and Joan Lockwood O'Donovan (Grand Rapids, MI: Eerdmans, 1999), 294–96.

23. Ford, *Political Murder*, 123.

24. Leon Friedman, ed., *The Law of War: A Documentary History*, vol. 1 (New York: Random House, 1972) 38, n.16.

25. Thomas Aquinas, *Commentary on the Sentences*, II, Dist. 44, quaest. 2 in *Aquinas, Political Writings* (Cambridge Texts in the History of Political Thought), ed. and trans. R. W. Dyson (Cambridge: Cambridge University Press, 2002), 74.

26. Thomas Aquinas, *Summa Theologica*, II-II, q.69, a.4.

27. Johnstone, "Political Assassination and Tyrannicide," 35, summarizing Aquinas, *Summa Theologica*, II-II, q.64, a.3.

28. Johnstone, "Political Assassination and Tyrannicide," 37.

29. Ford, *Political Murder*, 187.

30. The 100 ducat price for the pope was a relative steal given the fee for dispatching the Grand Turk (500 ducats) or the King of Spain (150 ducats).

31. Ford, *Political Murder*, 136.

32. Ward Thomas, "Norms and Security: The Case of International Assassination," *International Security* 25/1 (2000): 105–33.

33. Ford, *Political Murder*, 151.

34. Ibid., 151. Here Ford is relying on Quentin Skinner, *Foundations of Modern Political Thought*, vol. II: *The Age of Reformation* (Cambridge: University of Cambridge Press, 1978), 194–207.

35. Ford, *Political Murder*, 152.

36. William Stevenson, Jr., "Calvin and Political Issues," in *The Cambridge Companion to John Calvin*, ed. Donald McKim (Cambridge: Cambridge University Press, 2004), 173–87 at 182–83.

37. John Calvin, *Institutes of Christian Religion*, II, chap. 8.

38. Ibid., IV, chap. 20, sec. 31.

39. George Sabine, *A History of Political Theory*, 4th ed. rev. by Thomas Thorson (Hinsdale, IL: Dryden Press, 1973), 344.

40. Ford, *Political Murder*, 156–57.

41. Edmund Dickerman, "The Conversion of Henry IV," *Catholic Historical Review* 63/1 (1977): 1–13.

42. Johnstone, "Political Assassination and Tyrannicide," 39–40, summarizing Suarez.

43. Ford, *Political Murder*, 157.

44. Emmerich de Vattel, "The Right of Peoples" (1758), reprinted in *The Classics of International Law*, trans. C. G. Fenwick (Washington, DC: Carnegie Institution, 1916), 288.

45. I rely here and throughout this subsection on Liguori to Johnstone, "Political Assassination and Tyrannicide," 40–42.

46. John McHugh and Charles Callan, *Moral Theology: A Complete Course*, vol. 2. Revised and Enlarged by Edward Farrell (New York: Joseph Wagner, 1958), 103–4.

47. Johnstone, "Political Assassination and Tyrannicide," 43.

48. Ibid., 43. Johnstone cites Asim Nanji, "Assassins," in *The Encyclopedia of Religion*, ed. Mircea Eliade (New York: Macmillan Publishing, 1987).

49. Ibid., 45.

50. Thomas, "Norms and Security," 112.

51. For example, deception is not the same as ambush. Ambush is generally seen as a fair tactic in war. Deception is frowned upon as unworthy and unfair for it violates the respect and fairness that ought to be part of war's restraints. If good faith is expressed then it should not be violated, for example, feigning a truce and then attacking. See Christine de Pizan, *The Book of Deeds of Arms and of Chivalry*, part III, chap. 13, in *The Ethics of War*, ed. Gregory Reichberg, Henrik Syse, and Endre Begby (Malden, MA: Blackwell Publishing, 2006), 220.

52. Steve Coll, "Remote Control," *New Yorker* (May 6, 2013), 76–79 at 76.

53. For one example, see Stephen Kershner, "The Moral Argument for a Policy of Assassination," *Reason Papers* 27 (2004): 43–66. Andrew Altman and Christopher Heath Wellman call for a reopening of the ban against all assassina-

tion on humanitarian grounds, not primarily to combat international terrorism. See "From Humanitarian Intervention to Assassination: Human Rights and Political Violence," *Ethics* 118 (2008): 228–57. A particularly helpful discussion of what is at stake in the new interest in the use of assassination as a tool in international security may be found in Ward Thomas, "The New Age of Assassination," *SAIS Review* 25/1 (2005): 27–39.

54. J. Bowyer Bell, "Assassination in International Politics," *International Studies Quarterly* 16/1 (1972): 59–82 at 60.

3. THE PROXIMATE CONTEXT

1. Gal Luft, "The Logic of Israel's Targeted Killing," *Middle East Quarterly* 10/1 (2003): 3–13.

2. The hijackings of commercial airliners and the attack on Israeli athletes at the 1972 Olympics were tragic events that received extensive live television coverage.

3. Jeremy Pressman, "The Second Intifada: Background and Causes of the Israeli Palestinian Conflict," *Journal of Conflict Studies* 23/2 (2003). http://journals.hil.unb.ca/index.php/JCS/article/view/220/378.

4. Daniel Byman, *A High Price: The Triumphs and Failures of Israeli Counterterrorism* (New York: Oxford University Press, 2013), 312.

5. The Israeli response to the Munich killings was "Operation Wrath of God." There was a good deal of international criticism that the Israeli actions were not motivated by self-defense but by revenge. Media reports at the time suggested there was no evidence that the Palestinians killed were planning future terrorist acts. The director of the Mossad (Israeli secret service) at the time claimed that the victims of the operation were planning additional attacks. That claim, made during an interview in Israel, has never been confirmed or denied by anyone else in the Israeli government. See Amos Guiora, *Legitimate Target: A Criteria-Based Approach to Targeted Killing* (Oxford: Oxford University Press, 2013), 66.

6. In the first Intifada the ratio of Palestinian to Israeli fatalities was 25 to 1, while in the second Intifada the ratio was reduced to 3 to 1. This reflects the changed weaponry employed by the Palestinians.

7. From September 2000 to September 2001 at least forty killings of middle- and high-level Palestinian activists took place. None were identified as Fatah

members but they came from Hamas, Palestinian Islamic Jihad, Tanzim, Al-Aqsa Martyrs Brigade, and the PFLP. As noted above, Israel had committed targeted killings previously, but the frequency of the practice increased dramatically in response to the second Intifada.

8. Byman, *A High Price*, 314.
9. Ibid., 315.
10. Luft, "Logic of Israel's Targeted Killing," 3.
11. As reported in Byman, *A High Price*, 313.
12. Luft, "Logic of Israel's Targeted Killing," 3–4.
13. Steven David, "Israel's Policy of Targeted Killing," *Ethics in International Affairs (EIA)* 17/1 (2003): 111–26 at 112.
14. Ibid., 114.
15. Ibid., 114.
16. Yael Stein, "By Any Name Illegal and Immoral," *EIA* 17/1 (2003): 127–37 at 127.
17. Ibid., 129.
18. Ibid., 130
19. Ibid., 135.
20. Ibid., 132.
21. Ibid., 132, quoting David, "Israel's Policy of Targeted Killing," at 121 and 122.
22. Ibid., 132, quoting David, "Israel's Policy of Targeted Killing," at 123.
23. Ibid., 132. Byman, *A High Price*, 313, also acknowledges that the targeted killing policy is very popular with the Israeli public and that Israeli politicians are not unaware of the public's desire for revenge against terrorists, nor the satisfaction that comes when the Israeli government strikes back.
24. Ibid., 133.
25. Steven David, "If Not Combatants, Certainly Not Civilians," *EIA* 17/1 (2003): 138–40 at 138.
26. Ibid., 139.
27. Ibid., 140.
28. Michael Gross, "Fighting by Other Means in the Mideast: A Critical Analysis of Israel's Assassination Policy," *Political Studies* 51 (2003): 350–68 at 352.
29. Ibid., 351.
30. Ibid., 364.

31. Daniel Statman, "The Morality of Assassination: A Response to Gross," *Political Studies* 51 (2003): 775–79 at 777.

32. Ibid., 778.

33. Daniel Statman, "Targeted Killing," *Theoretical Inquiries in Law* 5/1 (2004): 179–98.

34. Ibid., 184.

35. Ibid., 187.

36. Ibid., 191.

37. Ibid., 187.

38. Ibid., 195.

39. Ibid., 196.

40. Neither Israel nor the United States accepted the revisions but many commentators claim that the changed conventions carry the weight of customary international law.

41. Michael Gross, "Assassination and Targeted Killing: Law Enforcement, Execution or Self-Defense?" *Journal of Applied Philosophy* 23/3 (2006): 323–35 at 324. The essay has been reprinted in David Rodin, ed., *War, Torture and Terrorism: Ethics and War in the 21st Century* (Cambridge: Blackwell Publishing, 2007), 83–95.

42. Ibid., 330.

43. Ibid., 332.

44. Ibid., 332–33.

45. Daniel Statman, "Can Just War Theory Justify Targeted Killing? Three Possible Models," in *Targeted Killing: Law and Morality in an Asymmetrical World,* ed. Claire Finkelstein, Jens David Ohlin, and Andrew Altman (Oxford: Oxford University Press, 2012), 90–111.

46. Ibid., 90–91.

47. Ibid., 95.

48. Ibid., 95–97.

49. Ibid., 99.

50. Ibid., 103.

51. Ibid., 104–5.

52. Ibid., 106.

53. Amos Guiora, "Targeted Killing as Active Self-Defense," *Case Western Reserve Journal of International Law* 36 (2004): 319–34 at 324.

54. Ibid., 323.

55. Ibid., 329.

56. Ibid., 328.

57. Ibid., 334.

58. Asa Kasher and Amos Yadlin, "Assassination and Preventive Killing," *SAIS Review* 25/1 (2005): 41–57 at 44.

59. Ibid., 45.

60. Ibid., 45.

61. Ibid., 48–49.

62. Avishai Margalit and Michael Walzer, "Israel: Civilians and Combatants," *New York Review of Books* 56/8 (May 14, 2009), have rightly challenged Kasher and Yadlin for fudging the combatant/noncombatant distinction, the point of which is to limit war only to those "who have the capacity to injure" one another. Soldiers ought never intend to kill civilians, "and that active intention can be made manifest only through the risks the soldiers themselves accept in order to reduce the risk to civilians."

63. David Kretzmer, "Targeted Killing of Suspected Terrorists: Extra-Judicial Executions or Legitimate Means of Defence?" *European Journal of International Law* 16/2 (2005): 171–212 at 174.

64. Ibid., 179.

65. Ibid., 182.

66. Ibid., 189.

67. Ibid., 191.

68. Ibid., 193.

69. Ibid., 202.

70. Ibid., 211.

71. Ibid., 212.

72. Tamar Meisels, "Combatants—Lawful and Unlawful," *Law and Philosophy* 26 (2007): 31–65 at 32.

73. Ibid., 35.

74. Ibid., 46.

75. Ibid., 48.

76. Ibid., 48.

77. Ibid., 57.

78. Ibid., 57.

79. High Court of Justice 769/02, *The Public Committee against Torture in Israel v. The Government of Israel*, 16. (References to the decision will be by paragraph, not page number.)

80. Ibid., 18.

81. Ibid., 21.
82. Ibid., 25.
83. Ibid., 26.
84. Ibid., 29.
85. See note 40.
86. Ibid., 31.
87. Ibid., 32.
88. Ibid., 33.
89. Ibid., 34.
90. Ibid., 35.
91. Ibid., 37.
92. Ibid., 39.
93. Ibid., 40.
94. Ibid., 43.
95. Byman, *A High Price*, 52–53.
96. Byman recounts a story of the targeted killing of six Palestinian policemen that outraged IDF members since the action seemed to be done with little certainty that the targets were guilty of a crime. Ibid., 322.
97. Ibid., 316.

4. THE IMMEDIATE CONTEXT

1. Barack Obama, "Remarks by the President at the Acceptance of the Nobel Peace Prize" (December 10, 2009), 2. http://www.whitehouse.gov/the-press-office/remarks-president-acceptance-nobel-peace-prize.
2. Ibid., 3
3. Daniel Klaidman, *Kill or Capture* (Boston: Houghton Mifflin Harcourt, 2012), 117.
4. Ibid., 118.
5. Barack Obama, "Remarks by the President on National Security" (May 21, 2009). http://www.whitehouse.gov/the-press-office/remarks-president-national-security-5–21–09.
6. Klaidman, *Kill or Capture*, 21.
7. Ibid., 23.
8. Ibid., 40–42.
9. Ibid., 118.

10. Ibid., 120.

11. Ibid., 265.

12. Ibid., 262.

13. Ibid., 262.

14. Michael Isikoff, "Justice Department Memo Reveals Legal Case for Drone Strikes on Americans" (January 28, 2013). http://investigations.nbcnews.com/_news/2013/02/04/16843014-justice-department-memo-reveals-legal-case-for-drone-strikes-on-americans.

15. Department of Justice White Paper, "Lawfulness of a Lethal Operation Directed Against a U.S. Citizen Who Is a Senior Operational Leader of al-Qaida or an Associated Force," 1. http://msnbcmedia.msn.com/i/msnbc/sections/news/020413_DOJ_White_Paper.pdf.

16. Ibid., 1.

17. Rosa Brooks, "Death by Loophole," *Foreign Policy* (February 5, 2013). http://www.foreignpolicy.com/articles/2013/02/05/death_by_loophole.

18. Ibid.

19. A sampling of other public criticism includes David Cole, "How We Made Killing Easy," *NYR Blog* (February 6, 2013). http://www.nybooks.com/blogs/nyrblog/2013/feb/06/drones-killing-made-easy/; "President Obama, Did or Did You Not Kill Anwar al-Awlaki?" *Washington Post* (February 8, 2013). http://www.washingtonpost.com/opinions/president-obama-did-or-did-you-not-kill-anwar-al-awlaki/2013/02/08/0347f4de-70c9–11e2-a050-b83a7b35c4b5_story.html; Jameel Jaffer, "The Justice Department's White Paper on Targeted Killing," American Civil Liberties Union (February 4, 2013). https://www.aclu.org/blog/national-security/justice-departments-white-paper-targeted-killing.

20. Scott Shane and Mark Mazzetti, "White House Tactic for C.I.A. Bid Holds Back Drone Memos," *New York Times* (February 20, 2013). http://www.nytimes.com/2013/02/21/us/politics/strategy-seeks-to-ensure-bid-of-brennan-for-cia.html?pagewanted=all&_r=0.

21. James Downie, "The Justice Department's Chilling 'Targeted Killings' Memo," *Washington Post* (February 5, 2013). http://www.washingtonpost.com/blogs/post-partisan/wp/2013/02/05/justice-department-chilling-drone-white-paper/.

22. Shane and Mazzetti, "White House Tactic for C.I.A. Bid."

23. United States Senate Select Committee on Intelligence, "Open Hearing on the Nomination of John O. Brennan to Be Director of the Central Intelligence

Agency" (February 7, 2013). http://www.intelligence.senate.gov/130207/transcript.pdf.

24. Ibid., 57 (italics in original).

25. Ibid., 55–56.

26. United States Senate Select Committee on Intelligence, "Additional Prehearing Questions for Mr. John O. Brennan upon His Nomination to Be the Director of the Central Intelligence Agency," 24. http://www.intelligence.senate.gov/130207/prehearing.pdf.

27. Committee on Intelligence, "Open Hearing," 56.

28. Committee on Intelligence, "Additional Prehearing Questions," 28.

29. Isikoff, "Justice Department Memo."

30. Scott Shane and Charlie Savage, "Report on Targeted Killing Whets Appetite for Less Secrecy," *New York Times* (February 5, 2013). http://www.nytimes.com/2013/02/06/us/politics/obama-slow-to-reveal-secrets-on-targeted-killings.html?pagewanted=all&_r=0.

31. Harold Koh, "The Obama Administration and International Law" (March 25, 2010), 8. http://www.state.gov/s/l/releases/remarks/139119.htm.

32. Ibid., 8.

33. Klaidman, *Kill or Capture*, 219.

34. Ibid., 219–20.

35. John Brennan, "Strengthening Our Security by Adhering to Our Values and Laws," Program on Law and Security, Harvard Law School (September 16, 2011), 2. http://www.whitehouse.gov/the-press-office/2011/09/16/remarks-john-o-brennan-strengthening-our-security-adhering-our-values-an.

36. Ibid., 3.

37. Ibid., 3.

38. Jeh Charles Johnson, "National Security Law, Lawyers and Lawyering in the Obama Administration," Dean's Lecture at Yale Law School (February 22, 2012), 4. http://www.lawfareblog.com/2012/02/jeh-johnson-speech-at-yale-law-school/#.UtgqS18o7cs.

39. Ibid., 4–5.

40. Ibid., 5.

41. Ibid., 5 (italics in original). Later in the same year, on November 30, Johnson also gave a public speech at the Oxford Union that repeated some of what he said at Yale but broke no new ground in the administration's explanation or defense of the use of drones in targeted killing. The Oxford speech is available

at http://www.lawfareblog.com/2012/11/jeh-johnson-speech-at-the-oxford-union/#_ftn1.

42. Eric Holder, "Attorney General Eric Holder Speaks at Northwestern University School of Law" (March 5, 2012), 5. http://www.justice.gov/iso/opa/ag/speeches/2012/ag-speech-1203051.html.

43. Ibid., 5.

44. Ibid., 5.

45. Ibid., 6.

46. Ibid., 6.

47. John Brennan, "The Ethics and Efficacy of the President's Counterterrorism Strategy," Woodrow Wilson International Center for Scholars (April 30, 2012), 5. http://www.wilsoncenter.org/event/the-efficacy-and-ethics-us-counterterrorism-strategy/#.

48. Ibid., 5.

49. Ibid., 6.

50. Ibid., 6.

51. Ibid., 6.

52. Ibid., 7.

53. Ibid., 7.

54. Ibid., 7.

55. Ibid., 8.

56. Ibid., 9.

57. Ibid., 10.

58. Ibid., 11.

59. Barack Obama, "Remarks by the President at the National Defense University" (May 23, 2013), 5. http://www.whitehouse.gov/the-press-office/2013/05/23/remarks-president-national-defense-university.

60. Ibid., 5–6.

61. Ibid., 6.

62. Ibid., 6.

63. Ibid., 6.

64. Ibid., 7.

65. Ibid., 7.

66. Ibid., 7.

67. Ibid., 8.

68. Ibid., 8.

69. Ibid., 8.

70. Ibid., 6.

71. Scott Shane, "Election Spurred a Move to Codify U.S. Drone Policy," *New York Times* (November 24, 2012). http://www.nytimes.com/2012/11/25/world/white-house-presses-for-drone-rule-book.html?pagewanted=all&_r=0.

72. Greg Miller, Ellen Nakashima, and Karen DeYoung, "CIA Drone Strikes Will Get Pass in Counterterrorism 'Playbook,' Officials Say," *Washington Post* (January 19, 2013). http://www.washingtonpost.com/world/national-security/cia-drone-strikes-will-get-pass-in-counterterrorism-playbook-officials-say/2013/01/19/ca169a20–618d-11e2–9940–6fc488f3fecd_story.html.

73. Office of the Press Secretary, "U.S. Policy Standards and Procedures for the Use of Force in Counterterrorism Operations Outside the United States and Areas of Active Hostilities," White House (May 23, 2013). http://www.whitehouse.gov/the-press-office/2013/05/23/fact-sheet-us-policy-standards-and-procedures-use-force-counterterrorism.

74. Ibid., 1.

75. Ibid., 2.

76. Ibid., 3.

77. Kenneth Anderson and Benjamin Wittes, *Speaking the Law* (Stanford, CA: Hoover Institution Press, 2013), 160.

78. Ibid., 164.

79. Ibid., 165.

80. Ibid., 166.

81. Gregory McNeal, "Targeted Killing and Accountability," *Georgetown Law Journal* 102 (2014): 681–794 at 689. http://georgetownlawjournal.org/files/2014/03/McNeal-TargetedKilling.pdf.

82. Ibid., 701. McNeal's article examines the process for true targeted killings, that is, named killings, not signature strikes.

83. Ibid., 706.

84. International Committee of the Red Cross, "Interpretive Guidelines on the Notion of Direct Participation in Hostilities under International Humanitarian Law," *International Review of the Red Cross* 90/872 (2008): 991–1047 at 1007, n.109.

85. McNeal, "Targeted Killing and Accountability," 707.

86. Ibid., 707.

87. Ibid., 708.

88. Ibid., 709.

89. Ibid., n.133.

90. Ibid., 711–12.
91. Ibid., 717.
92. Ibid., 717–19.
93. Ibid., 715–16.
94. Ibid., 715.
95. Ibid., 721.
96. Ibid., n.188.
97. Ibid., 723.
98. Ibid., 724.
99. Ibid., 726.
100. Ibid., 727.
101. Ibid., 731.
102. Ibid., 734–35.
103. Ibid., 735.
104. Ibid., 738.
105. Ibid., 739.
106. Ibid., 740.
107. Ibid., 740–50.
108. Ibid., 750. "For example, in U.S. military operations in Afghanistan, if the amount of unavoidable collateral damage is low, the President has delegated decision-making authority to generals. If, however, the expected collateral damage is high, authorization is reserved for the President or the Secretary of Defense."

5. THE FUTURE CONTEXT

1. Michael J. Boyle, "The Costs and Consequences of Drone Warfare," *International Affairs* 89/1 (2013): 1–29 at 4. The author claims that in materials captured as a result of the lethal raid on Osama bin Laden's house there were clear indicators that bin Laden thought drone strikes were highly successful in killing the al-Qaida leadership. It should be noted that Boyle cites these benefits in order to rebut them as he is a critic of the present U.S. policy.
2. Bradley Jay Strawser, "Moral Predators: The Duty to Employ Uninhabited Aerial Vehicles," *Journal of Military Ethics* 9/4 (2010): 342–68.

3. Barack Obama, "Remarks by the President at the National Defense University" (May 23, 2013), 7. http://www.whitehouse.gov/the-press-office/2013/05/23/remarks-president-national-defense-university.

4. Brian Johnstone, "Noncombatant Immunity: The Origin of the Principle in Theology and Law," *Studia Moralia* 24 (1986): 115–48.

5. Michael Gross, "Assassination and Targeted Killing: Law Enforcement, Execution or Self-Defense?" in *War, Torture and Terrorism*, ed. David Rodin (Malden, MA: Blackwell Publishing, 2007), 83–95, at 83.

6. Jeff McMahan in live chat on "The Ethics of Drone Warfare." http://www.newyorker.com/news/news-desk/live-chat-the-ethics-of-drone-warfare.

7. For a detailed account of the entire process of formulating the list of those subject to targeted killings, see Gregory McNeal, "Targeted Killing and Accountability," *Georgetown Law Journal* (March 2014): 681–794. http://www.georgetownlawjournal.org/files/2014/03/McNeal-TargetedKilling.pdf.

8. Center for Civilians in Conflict and Columbia Law School Human Rights Clinic, *The Civilian Impact of Drones: Unexamined Costs, Unanswered Questions* (New York: Center for Civilians in Conflict, 2012), 8. http://civiliansinconflict.org/resources/pub/the-civilian-impact-of-drones.

9. Richard Haass, "The President Has Too Much Latitude to Order Drone Strikes," *Wall Street Journal* (February 18, 2013). http://www.cfr.org/drones/president-has-too-much-latitude-order-drone-strikes/p30021; Jesselyn Radack, "Brennan's (FAKE) Criteria for Drone Strikes," *Daily Kos* (May 1, 2012). http://www.dailykos.com/story/2012/05/01/1087797/-Brennan-s-FAKE-Criteria-for-Drone-Strikes.

10. Micah Zenko, "Targeted Killings and Signature Strikes," Council on Foreign Relations (July 16, 2012), 2, quoting an unidentified Bush administration official. http://blogs.cfr.org/zenko/2012/07/16/targeted-killings-and-signature-strikes/.

11. Ibid., 3–4.

12. Kenneth Roth, "What Rules Should Govern US Drone Attacks?" *New York Review of Books* (April 4, 2013). http://www.nybooks.com/articles/archives/2013/apr/04/what-rules-should-govern-us-drone-attacks/. Recall that John Brennan, then White House counterterrorism chief, gave a speech on April 30, 2012, in which he stated that to be targeted a person should be an operative "in the midst of actually training for or planning to carry out attacks against U.S. interests." The criticism here is not so much to Brennan's stated policy but to the actual practice of targeting that seems less restrictive.

13. Boyle, "The Costs and Consequences," 8.

14. Gregory Johnsen, "Nothing Says 'Sorry Our Drones Hit Your Wedding Party' Like $800,000 and Some Guns," on Buzzfeed.com (September 5, 2014). http://www.buzzfeed.com/gregorydjohnsen/wedding-party-drone-strike#335cm8y. See also Christine Hauser, "The Aftermath of Drone Strikes on a Wedding Convoy in Yemen," *Lede, New York Times Blog* (December 19, 2013). http://thelede.blogs.nytimes.com/2013/12/19/the-aftermath-of-drone-strikes-on-a-wedding-convoy-in-yemen/.

15. Stimson Center, "Recommendations and Report on the Task Force on Drone Policy," cochairs, John Abizaid and Rosa Brooks; project director, Rachel Stohl (Washington, DC: Stimson Center, 2014), 36. http://www.stimson.org.

16. International Human Rights and Conflict Resolution Clinic at Stanford and Global Justice Clinic at NYU School of Law, *Living Under Drones: Death, Injury, and Trauma to Civilians from U.S. Drone Practices in Pakistan* (September 2012). http://www.livingunderdrones.org/report/.

17. Roth, "What Rules Should Govern?"; and "Statement of Shared Concerns Regarding U.S. Drone Strikes and Targeted Killings," signed by ten organizations engaged in human rights work, including the American Civil Liberties Union, Amnesty International, and Human Rights Watch. http://www.hrw.org/sites/default/files/related_material/4-11-13_US_LetterToPresidentObama OnTargetedKillings.pdf.

18. *"When I use a word," Humpty Dumpty said in rather a scornful tone, "it means what I choose it to mean, neither more nor less." "The question is," said Alice, "whether you CAN make words mean so many different things."*
"The question is," said Humpty Dumpty, "which is to be master—that's all."
(Lewis Carroll)

19. David Cole, "How We Made Killing Easy," *New York Review of Books* (February 6, 2013). http://www.nybooks.com/blogs/nyrblog/2013/feb/06/drones-killing-made-easy/.

20. Amitai Etzioni, "The Great Drone Debate," *Military Review* (March/April 2013): 5.

21. Ibid., 6.

22. Roth, "What Rules Should Govern?"

23. Michael Walzer, *Just and Unjust Wars* (New York: Basic Books, 1977), 143.

24. Fernando Teson, "Targeted Killing in War and Peace: A Philosophical Analysis," in *Targeted Killings: Law and Morality in an Asymmetrical World*,

ed. Claire Finkelstein, Jens David Ohlin, and Andrew Altman (Oxford: Oxford University Press, 2012), 403–33 at 417.

25. International Committee of the Red Cross, *Interpretive Guidance on the Notion of Direct Participation in Hostilities* (Geneva: ICRC, 2009). https://www.icrc.org/eng/assets/files/other/icrc-002-0990.pdf.

26. Robert Chesney, "Who May Be Killed? Anwar al-Awlaki as a Case Study in the International Legal Regulation of Lethal Force," *Yearbook of International Humanitarian Law* 13 (February 2, 2011): 48, University of Texas Law, Public Law Research Paper No. 189. http://papers.ssrn.com/sol3/papers.cfm?abstract_id=1754223.

27. Ibid.

28. This list reflects the way Israel understands the meaning of direct engagement in terrorist activity. See Asa Kasher and Amos Yadlin, "Assassination and Preventive Killing," *SAIS Review of International Affairs* 25 (2005): 41–57 at 48–49.

29. James Keenan, "Cooperation, Principle of," in *New Dictionary of Catholic Social Thought,* ed. Judith Dwyer (Collegeville, MN: Liturgical Press, 1994), 232–35.

30. John Brennan, "The Ethics and Efficacy of the President's Counterterrorism Strategy," Woodrow Wilson International Center for Scholars (April 30, 2012), 7. http://www.wilsoncenter.org/event/the-efficacy-and-ethics-us-counterterrorism-strategy/#.

31. Ibid., 8.

32. Benjamin Wittes, "Clarification from Tom Malinowski," *Lawfare Blog* (November 4, 2010). http://www.lawfareblog.com/2010/11/reflections-on-malinowskis-clarification/.

33. Chesney, "Who May Be Killed," 56.

34. Ibid., 56.

35. John Tirman, *The Death of Others* (Oxford: Oxford University Press, 2011); Daniel Rothbart and Karina Korostelina, *Why They Die* (Ann Arbor: University of Michigan Press, 2011).

36. A study by the International Committee for the Red Cross analyzed twentieth-century wars and put the ratio at 10 civilian deaths to 1 combatant death. See http://www.icrc.org/eng/assets/files/other/irrc-872-wenger-mason.pdf.

37. Robert Wright, "The Price of Assassination," *New York Times* (April 13, 2010). http://opinionator.blogs.nytimes.com/2010/04/13/title-2.

38. Stimson Center, "Task Force Report," n. 21.

39. Charli Carpenter and Lina Shaikhouni, "Don't Fear the Reaper," *Foreign Policy* (June 7, 2011). http://foreignpolicy.com/2011/06/07/dont-fear-the-reaper/.

40. Ibid.

41. Joshua Foust and Ashley S. Boyle, "The Strategic Context of Lethal Drones," American Security Project (August 16, 2012), 6. http://www.americansecurityproject.org/the-strategic-context-of-lethal-drones-a-framework-for-discussion/.

42. Micah Zenko, "10 Things You Didn't Know about Drones," *Foreign Policy* (March/April, 2012). http://www.foreignpolicy.com/articles/2012/02/27/10_things_you_didnt_know_about_drones.

43. Daniel Byman, "Why Drones Work," *Foreign Affairs* (July/August 2013), 4. http://www.foreignaffairs.com/articles/139453/daniel-byman/why-drones-work.

44. One prominent drone critic who cites the Kilcullen/Exum figure is Mary Ellen O'Connell, "Flying Blind," *America* (March 5, 2010). http://www.americamagazine.org/content/article.cfm?article_id=12179.

45. Center for Civilians in Conflict, *The Civilian Impact*, 2.

46. Boyle, "Costs and Consequences," 7.

47. Singh's original study appeared on the website www.lawfareblog.com in July 2013. An updated version was published in August of this year in the *New Republic*. See Ritika Singh, "Drone Strikes Kill Innocent People. Why Is It So Hard to Know How Many?" http://www.newrepublic.com/article/115353/civilian-casualties-drone-strikes-why-we-know-so-little.

48. Ibid.

49. Jakob Kellenberger, president of the International Committee for the Red Cross, acknowledged in a 2011 speech that because drones have "enhanced real-time aerial surveillance possibilities," they "thereby [allow] belligerents to carry out their attacks more precisely against military objectives and thus reduce civilian casualties and damage to civilian objects—in other words, to exercise greater precaution in attack." Quoted in Amitai Etzioni, "The Great Drone Debate," *Military Review* 93/2 (March/April 2013): 2–13 at 7.

50. Shashank Bengali and David Cloud, "U.S. Drone Strikes Up Sharply in Afghanistan," *Los Angeles Times* (February 21, 2012), 2. http://articles.latimes.com/2013/feb/21/world/la-fg-afghanistan-drones-20130222; Mark Jacobson, "Five Myths about Obama's Drone War," *Washington Post* (February 8, 2013),

2. https://www.washingtonpost.com/opinions/five-myths-about-obamas-drone-war/2013/02/08/c9ef3d78-708c-11e2-a050-b83a7b35c4b5_story.html.

51. Rosa Brooks, "Take Two Drones and Call Me in the Morning," *Foreign Policy* (September 12, 2012), 1. http://foreignpolicy.com/2012/09/13/take-two-drones-and-call-me-in-the-morning/.

52. Carpenter and Shaikhouni, "Don't Fear the Reaper," 3.

53. Mark Bowden, "The Killing Machines," *Atlantic* (September 2013). http://www.theatlantic.com/magazine/archive/2013/09/the-killing-machines-how-to-think-about-drones/309434/.

54. Stimson Center, "Task Force Report," 25: "The empirical evidence suggests that the number of civilians killed is small compared to the civilian deaths typically associated with other weapons delivery systems (including manned aircraft)."

55. Andreas Wenger and Simon J. A. Mason, "The Civilianization of Armed Conflict: Trends and Implications," *International Review of the Red Cross* 90/872 (December 2008). http://www.icrc.org/eng/assets/files/other/irrc-872-wenger-mason.pdf.

56. Audrey Kurth Cronin, "Why Drones Fail," *Foreign Affairs* (July/August 2013), 3. http://www.foreignaffairs.com/articles/139454/audrey-kurth-cronin/why-drones-fail.

57. Center for Civilians in Conflict and Columbia Law School Human Rights Clinic, *The Civilian Impact of Drones: Unexamined Costs, Unanswered Questions* (2012); Stanford/NYU, *Living under Drones*; Amnesty International, "'Will I Be Next?': U.S. Drone Strikes in Pakistan" (2013); Human Rights Watch, "'Between a Drone and Al-Qaeda': The Civilian Cost of U.S. Targeted Killings in Yemen" (2013).

58. Stanford/NYU, *Living under Drones*.

59. Boyle, "Cost and Consequences," 21.

60. Roth, "What Rules Should Govern?"

61. Maryann Cusimano Love, "White House: Drone Program 'Ethical,' 'Legal' and 'Wise.' Is It?" *Washington Post* (February 5, 2013). http://www.faithstreet.com/onfaith/2013/02/06/white-house-drone-program-legal-ethical-and-wise-is-it/11959.

62. Cole, "How We Made Killing Easy."

63. Ibid.; see also Roth, "What Rules Should Govern?"

64. Gerald Powers as quoted in Dennis Sadowski, "In the Face of Secrecy, Drone Warfare Faces Barrage of Moral Questions," Catholic News Service (February 15, 2013). http://www.catholicnews.com/data/stories/cns/1300674.htm.

65. Benjamin Friedman, "Etzioni and the Great Drone Debate," *National Interest* (October 5, 2011). http://nationalinterest.org/blog/the-skeptics/etzioni-the-great-drone-debate-5982.

66. Center for Civilians in Conflict, *The Civilian Impact of Drones*, 69.

67. Jo Becker and Eric Schmitt, "Secret 'Kill List' Proves a Test of Obama's Principles and Will," *New York Times* (May 29, 2012). http://www.nytimes.com/2012/05/29/world/obamas-leadership-in-war-on-al-qaeda.html?pagewanted=all&_r=0.

68. Byman, "Why Drones Work," 1.

69. Gal Luft, "The Logic of Israel's Targeted Killing," *Middle East Quarterly* 10/1 (2003): 3–13, and Steven David, "Israel's Policy of Targeted Killing," *EIA* 17/1 (2003): 111–26 make the point about the impact an effective policy of targeted killing can have upon terrorist organizations.

70. Stimson Center, "Task Force Report," 11.

71. Stimson Center, "Task Force Report," 31.

72. Micah Zenko, "The Seven Deadly Sins of John Brennan," *Foreign Policy* (September 18, 2012). http://www.foreignpolicy.com/articles/2012/09/18/the_seven_deadly_sins_of_john_brennan/.

73. Jenna Jordan, "When Heads Roll: Assessing the Effectiveness of Leadership Decapitation," *Security Studies* 18 (2009): 719–55.

74. Wright, "Price of Assassination."

75. Cronin, "Why Drones Fail," 2.

76. Bowden, "Killing Machines."

77. Center for Civilians in Conflict, *The Civilian Impact of Drones*, 23, quoting Robert Grenier, former head of the CIA Counterterrorism Center.

78. Stimson Center, "Task Force Report," 30.

79. Cronin, "Why Drones Fail," 3.

80. Stimson Center, "Task Force Report," 31. According to a 2012 Pew survey only 17 percent of Pakistanis approved of U.S. drone strikes. In Turkey 81 percent were against the strikes, in Jordan 85 percent, and in Egypt 89 percent. In Europe there were majorities in Poland, Germany, France, Spain, and Greece opposed to American drone strikes. This despite the 2008 pledge of President Obama when he was running for office that he would restore the reputation of the United States abroad. See Cronin, "Why Drones Fail," 5.

81. Rosa Brooks, "The Constitutional and Counterterrorism Implications of Targeted Killing," Testimony before the Senate Judiciary Subcommittee on the Constitution, Civil Rights, and Human Rights (April 23, 2013), 7. http://scholarship.law.georgetown.edu/cgi/viewcontent.cgi?article=1114&context=cong.

82. Boyle, "Costs and Consequences," 3.

83. Ibid., 15.

84. Boyle points out that while much is made of the Pakistani government's "tacit consent" to U.S. drone strikes, there is a notable difference in the government's view of attacks that remove high-ranking terrorists that might threaten Pakistan internally and the increased number of CIA attacks that kill low-level militants. Killing well-known and widely acknowledged terrorists receives a very different reaction than the deaths of those whose terrorist connections are weak or disputable.

85. Ibid., 19.

86. Micah Zenko, "Reforming U.S. Drone Strike Policies," Council on Foreign Relations Special Report No. 65 (January 2013), 11. http://www.cfr.org/wars-and-warfare/reforming-us-drone-strike-policies/p29736.

87. Stimson Center, "Task Force Report," 11.

88. Byman, "Why Drones Work," 8.

89. Greg Miller, "Increased U.S. Drone Strikes in Pakistan Killing Few High Value Militants," *Washington Post* (February 21, 2011). http://www.washingtonpost.com/wp-dyn/content/article/2011/02/20/AR2011022002975.html.

90. Bowden, "Killing Machines."

91. Cronin, "Why Drones Fail," 4.

92. Brooks, "Constitutional and Counterterrorism Implications," 6. The BIJ has reported that only 4 percent of drone attack victims in Pakistan have been positively identified as being part of al-Qaida. http://www.thebureauinvestigates.com/2014/10/16/only-4-of-drone-victims-in-pakistan-named-as-al-qaeda-members/.

93. Daniel Brunstetter, "Can We Wage a Just Drone War?" *Atlantic* (July 2012). http://www.theatlantic.com/technology/print/2012/07/can-we-wage-a-just-drone-war/260055/.

94. Stimson Center, "Task Force Report," 13.

95. Zenko, "Reforming U.S. Drone Strike Policies," 24.

96. Haass, "President Has Too Much Latitude."

97. Peter Singer and Thomas Wright, "Big Bets and Black Swans—A Presidential Briefing Book," Brookings Institution (January 2014). http://www.brookings.edu/~/media/Programs/foreign policy/BBBS/BigBets_BlackSwans_2014.pdf.

98. Diane Vavrichek, "The Future of Drone Strikes," CNA: Analysis and Solutions Occasional Papers (September 2014), 48. http://www.cna.org/sites/default/files/research/COP-2014-U-008318-Final.pdf.

99. Zenko, "Reforming U.S. Drone Strike Policies," 5.

100. Brooks, "Constitutional and Counterterrorism Implications," 15.

101. Stimson Center, "Task Force Report," 31.

102. Ibid., 37.

103. Boyle, "Costs and Consequences," 25.

104. Marie Dennis, co-president of Pax Christi, the Catholic peace organization, as quoted in "In the Face of Secrecy."

105. Roth, "What Rules Should Govern?"

106. William Pfaff, "Anonymous Murder from a Safe Distance," *Truthdig* (April 9, 2013). http://www.truthdig.com/report/item/anonymous_murder_from_a_safe_distance_20130409.

107. Roth, "What Rules Should Govern?"

108. Wright, "Price of Assassination," 8.

109. Bowden, "Killing Machines."

110. Stimson Center, "Task Force Report," 15; see also 43–45.

111. Peter Singer, "Do Drones Undermine Democracy?" *New York Times* (January 21, 2012), 2. http://www.nytimes.com/2012/01/22/opinion/sunday/do-drones-undermine-democracy.html?pagewanted=all&_r=0.

112. Ibid., 3.

113. A February 2012 poll reported in the *Washington Post* showed an 83 percent approval rating of the drone policy. Scott Wilson and Jon Cohen, "Poll Finds Broad Support for Obama's Counterterrorism Policies," *Washington Post* (February 8, 2012). http://www.washingtonpost.com/politics/poll-finds-broad-support-for-obamas-counterterrorism-policies/2012/02/07/gIQAFrSEyQ_story.html.

114. Firmin DeBrabander, "Drones and the Democracy Disconnect," *New York Times* (September 14, 2014), 2. http://opinionator.blogs.nytimes.com/2014/09/14/drones-and-the-democracy-disconnect/.

115. Andrew Bacevich has been an early observer of the gap between the military and civilians in contemporary America. See his *Breach of Trust: How*

Americans Failed Their Soldiers and Their Country (New York: Metropolitan Books, 2013). More recently James Fallows made a similar point in "The Tragedy of the American Military," *Atlantic* (January/February 2015). http://www.theatlantic.com/features/archive/2014/12/the-tragedy-of-the-american-military/383516/.

116. DeBrabander, "Drones and Democracy," 5.

117. Ibid., 6.

118. Center for Civilians in Conflict, *The Civilian Impact of Drones*, 68.

119. Roth, "What Rules Should Govern?"; Lincoln Caplan, "The Targeted Killing Memo and the Problems of Secret law," *New York Times* (February 7, 2013). http://takingnote.blogs.nytimes.com/2013/02/07/the-targeted-killing-memo-and-the-problem-of-secret-law/?_r=0; Singer and Wright, "Big Bets"; Radack, "Brennan's (FAKE) Criteria."

120. Jameel Jaffer and Nathan Freed Wessler, "The C.I.A.'s Misuse of Secrecy," *New York Times* (April 29, 2012). http://www.nytimes.com/2012/04/30/opinion/the-cias-misuse-of-secrecy.html.

121. Ibid.

122. The "Statement of Shared Concerns" by various human rights groups provides a more detailed exposition of the information that ought to be shared for the sake of transparency in our American democracy.

123. Recall the overview of the process in the previous chapter.

124. Cole, "How We Made Killing Easy."

125. Stimson Center, "Task Force Report," 43.

126. Micah Zenko, "Policy Innovation Memorandum No. 31," Council on Foreign Relations (April 16, 2013), 1. http://www.cfr.org/drones/transferring-cia-drone-strikes-pentagon/p30434.

127. Stimson Center, "Task Force Report," 43. The CIA could still have the ability to conduct lethal covert actions in very rare circumstances if there was an immediate threat to the U.S. homeland or American outposts abroad. Such actions would need to be authorized by a specific presidential finding in each unusual circumstance.

128. FISA is the acronym for Foreign Intelligence Surveillance Act, a law passed in 1978 that empowered the Chief Justice of the U.S. Supreme Court to appoint select Federal District Court judges to hear and rule on government requests for wiretap and other surveillance measures. The FISA court grants warrants to be used when a foreign power or agent of that power is involved. The judges serve on a rotating basis in secret sessions held in Washington, DC, to

hear government requests. Rejection of a government request has proven to be exceedingly rare, although there are modifications of a request on occasion.

129. Jeh Johnson, "A 'Drone Court': Some Pros and Cons," Center on National Security at Fordham Law School (March 18, 2013), 1. http://www.lawfareblog.com/2013/03/jeh-johnson-speech-on-a-drone-court-some-pros-and-cons/.

130. Jack Goldsmith, "U.S. Needs a Rulebook for Secret Warfare," *Washington Post* (February 5, 2013). http://www.washingtonpost.com/opinions/us-needs-rules-of-engagement-for-secret-warfare/2013/02/05/449f786e-6a78-11e2-95b3-272d604a10a3_story.html.

131. According to the Pew Research Center, the opposition to drones in Britain, Germany, Poland, France, Italy, Czech Republic, Spain, Japan, and Greece outnumbers support, in some cases dramatically so. Among significant allies in the region Turkey (81 percent), Jordan (85 percent), Lebanon (69 percent), and Egypt (89 percent) all show widespread opposition to U.S. policy. In Pakistan the support of those holding a favorable view of the United States under President Obama has shrunk to 12 percent, which is lower than the 19 percent who viewed the United States positively when George Bush was still president. See the June 13, 2012, report of the Global Attitudes Project at the Pew Research site: http://www.pewglobal.org/2012/06/13/global-opinion-of-obama-slips-international-policies-faulted/.

132. Eli McCarthy, "What Are Drones Doing to Us?," *America* (April 2, 2013). http://americamagazine.org/content/all-things/what-are-drones-doing-us.

INDEX